General editor: Graham H...ll

1·50

Brodie's Notes on W...

Antony and Cleopatra

W. Baker M. Phil. Ph. D.
Formerly Senior Lecturer in English, West Midlands College, and currently
Associate Professor, Northern Illinois University, USA

MACMILLAN

First published by James Brodie Ltd
This revised edition first published 1991
by Pan Books Ltd

Reprinted 1992 by
THE MACMILLAN PRESS LTD
Houndmills, Basingstoke, Hampshire RG21 2XS
and London
Companies and representatives
throughout the world

ISBN 0-333-58169-5

Printed in Great Britain by
Clays Ltd, St Ives plc, Bungay, Suffolk

Contents

References in these Notes are to the
Arden Shakespeare: Antony and Cleopatra,
but as references are also given to particular acts
and scenes, the Notes may be used with any
edition of the play.

Preface

This student revision aid is based on the principle that in any close examination of Shakespeare's plays 'the text's the thing'. Seeing a performance, or listening to a tape or record of a performance, is essential and is in itself a valuable and stimulating experience in understanding and appreciation. However, a real evaluation of Shakespeare's greatness, of his universality and of the nature of his literary and dramatic art, can only be achieved by constant application to the texts of the plays themselves. These revised editions of Brodie's Notes are intended to supplement that process through detailed critical commentary.

The first aim of each book is to fix the whole play in the reader's mind by providing a concise summary of the plot, relating it back, where appropriate, to its source or sources. Subsequently the book provides a summary of each scene, followed by *critical comments*. These may convey its importance in the dramatic structure of the play, creation of atmosphere, indication of character development, significance of figurative language etc, and they will also explain or paraphrase difficult words or phrases and identify meaningful references. At the end of each act revision questions are set to test the student's specific and broad understanding and appreciation of the play.

An extended critical commentary follows this scene by scene analysis. This embraces such major elements as characterization, imagery, the use of blank verse and prose, soliloquies and other aspects of the play which the editor considers need close attention. The paramount aim is to send the reader back to the text. The book concludes with a series of revision questions which require a detailed knowledge of the play; the first of these has notes by the editor of what *might* be included in a written answer. The intention is to stimulate and to guide; the whole emphasis of this commentary is to encourage the student's *involvement* in the play, to develop disciplined critical responses and thus promote personal enrichment through the imaginative experience of our greatest writer.

Graham Handley

Shakespeare and the Elizabethan Playhouse

William Shakespeare was born in Stratford-upon-Avon in 1564, and there are reasons to suppose that he came from a relatively prosperous family. He was probably educated at Stratford Grammar School and, at the age of eighteen, married Anne Hathaway, who was twenty-six. They had three children, a girl born shortly after their marriage, followed by twins in 1585 (the boy died in 1596). It seems likely that Shakespeare left for London shortly after a company of visiting players had visited Stratford in 1585, for by 1592 – according to the jealous testimony of one of his fellow-writers Robert Greene – he was certainly making his way both as actor and dramatist. The theatres were closed because of the plague in 1593; when they reopened Shakespeare worked with the Lord Chamberlain's Men, later the King's Men, and became a shareholder in each of the two theatres with which he was most closely associated, the Globe and the Blackfriars. He later purchased New Place, a considerable property in his home town of Stratford, to which he retired in 1611; there he entertained his great contemporary Ben Jonson (1572–1637) and the poet Michael Drayton (1563–1631). An astute businessman, Shakespeare lived comfortably in the town until his death in 1616.

This is a very brief outline of the life of our greatest writer, for little more can be said of him with certainty, though the plays – and poems – are living witness to the wisdom, humanity and many-faceted nature of the man. He was both popular and successful as a dramatist, perhaps less so as an actor. He probably began work as a dramatist in the late 1580s, by collaborating with other playwrights and adapting old plays, and by 1598 Francis Meres was paying tribute to his excellence in both comedy and tragedy. His first original play was probably *Love's Labour's Lost* (1590) and while the theatres were closed during the plague he wrote his narrative poems *Venus and Adonis* (1593) and *The Rape of Lucrece* (1594). The sonnets were almost certainly written in the 1590s though not published until 1609; the first 126 are apparently addressed to a young man who was his friend and patron, while the rest are concerned with the 'dark lady'.

The dating of Shakespeare's plays has exercised scholars ever since the publication of the First Folio (1623), which listed them as comedies, histories and tragedies. It seems more important to look at them chronologically as far as possible, in order to trace Shakespeare's considerable development as a dramatist. The first period, say to the middle of the 1590s, included such plays as *Love's Labour's Lost*, *The Comedy of Errors*, *Richard III*, *The Taming of the Shrew*, *Romeo and Juliet* and *Richard II*. These early plays embrace the categories listed in the First Folio, so that Shakespeare the craftsman is evident in his capacity for variety of subject and treatment. The next phase includes *A Midsummer Night's Dream*, *The Merchant of Venice*, *Henry IV Parts 1 and 2*, *Henry V* and *Much Ado About Nothing*, as well as *Julius Caesar*, *As You Like It* and *Twelfth Night*. These are followed, in the early years of the century, by his great tragic period: *Hamlet*, *Othello*, *King Lear* and *Macbeth*, with *Antony and Cleopatra* and *Coriolanus* belonging to 1607–09. The final phase embraces the romances (1610–13), *Cymbeline*, *The Tempest* and *The Winter's Tale* and the historical play *Henry VIII*.

Each of these revision aids will place the individual text under examination in the chronology of the remarkable dramatic output that spanned twenty years from the early 1590s to about 1613. The practical theatre for which Shakespeare wrote and acted derived from the inn courtyards in which performances had taken place, the few playhouses in his day being modelled on their structure. They were circular or hexagonal in shape, allowing the balconies and boxes around the walls full view of the stage. This large stage, which had no scenery, jutted out into the pit, the most extensive part of the theatre, where the poorer people – the 'groundlings' – stood. There was no roof (though the Blackfriars, used from 1608 onwards, was an indoor theatre) and thus bad weather meant no performance. Certain plays were acted at court, and these private performances normally marked some special occasion. Costumes, often rich ones, were used, and music was a common feature, with musicians on or under the stage; this sometimes had additional features, for example a trapdoor to facilitate the entry of a ghost. Women were barred by law from appearing on stage, and all female parts were played by boy actors; this undoubtedly explains the many instances in Shakespeare where a woman has to conceal her identity by disguising

herself as a man, e.g. Rosalind in *As You Like It*, Viola in *Twelfth Night*.

Shakespeare and his contemporaries often adapted their plays from sources in history and literature, extending an incident or a myth or creating a dramatic narrative from known facts. They were always aware of their own audiences, and frequently included topical references, sometimes of a satirical flavour, which would appeal to – and be understood by – the ground-lings as well as their wealthier patrons who occupied the boxes. Shakespeare obviously learned much from his fellow dramatists and actors, being on good terms with many of them. Ben Jonson paid generous tribute to him in the lines prefaced to the First Folio of Shakespeare's plays:

Thou art a monument without a tomb,
And art alive still, while thy book doth live
And we have wits to read, and praise to give.

Among his contemporaries were Thomas Kyd (1558–94) and Christopher Marlowe (1564–93). Kyd wrote *The Spanish Tragedy*, the revenge motif here foreshadowing the much more sophisticated treatment evident in *Hamlet*, while Marlowe evolved the 'mighty line' of blank verse, a combination of natural speech and elevated poetry. The quality and variety of Shakespeare's blank verse owes something to the innovatory brilliance of Marlowe but carries the stamp of individuality, richness of association, technical virtuosity and, above all, the genius of imaginative power.

The texts of Shakespeare's plays are still rich sources for scholars, and the editors of these revision aids have used the Arden editions of Shakespeare, which are regarded as pre-eminent for their scholarly approach. They are strongly recommended for advanced students, but other editions, like The New Penguin Shakespeare, The New Swan, The Signet are all good annotated editions currently available. A reading list of selected reliable works on the play being studied is provided at the end of each commentary and students are advised to turn to these as their interest in the play deepens.

Literary terms used in these Notes

alliteration Repetitive sound sequences. The term is usually applied to consonants used close together and beginning with the same letter, as in 'The barge she sat in, like a burnish'd throne/Burn'd on the water (II, 2).

allusions A direct or indirect reference in the text of *Antony and Cleopatra* to another literary work or passage. Allusions also refer to geographical, political, historical, philosophical, religious references within the text. Thus, for example, Philo's reference to 'plated Mars', in the opening lines of the play, is an allusion to (1) war (2) the Roman God of War.

anticipatory image An image which anticipates what is to happen, e.g. Philo's 'plated Mars' above anticipates scenes of war in *Antony and Cleopatra*.

aphorism A short comment containing a general truism, e.g. 'Art is long, life is short.'

apostrophe A direct address to an absent person or thing.

assonance The repetition of similar or identical vowel sounds, as in 'The people love *me*, and the *sea* is mine' (II, 1).

blank verse Unrhymed lines of **iambic pentameter**, the verse form largely used by Shakespeare.

caesura A pause in the poetic line, e.g. Caesar's 'A greater crack. The round world' (V, 1).

conceits 'A combination of dissimilar images, or discovery of . . . resemblances in things apparently unlike' (Dr Johnson), e.g. 'flint' and 'hardness' and 'fault' (IV, 9).

couplets A pair of rhymed lines.

duosyllabic The emphasis on two syllables.

euphemism To speak well. Used in the sense of making unpleasant events or happenings less disagreeable, e.g. for death – 'to pass away'.

euphuism Elaboration, a flowery way of saying something.

hyperbole Excessive exaggeration, e.g. Cleopatra's comment in V,2 'His face was as the heavens.'

hypermetric A line containing additional syllables or feet.

iambic pentameters A poetic line of five feet with a light followed by a stressed syllable. Shakespeare's basic poetic line.

imagery A complicated term having three basic areas of meaning: (1) used as 'images' to refer to all the many references in the play; (2) used in a narrower sense to refer to descriptions of visual objects such as the stars, the sun, the moon, water; (3) the metaphors and similes in the play.

invocation A reference to a deity or spirit, e.g. Antony's references to 'The shirt of Nessus' and Hercules in IV,12.

irony Basically the difference between what is asserted, or appears to be, and what actually is. There are various forms: (1) dramatic irony relates to situations in the play in which the audience shares with the dramatist knowledge of which a character is ignorant. For example in Act IV we know that Cleopatra isn't dead, though Antony believes that she is; (2) verbal irony refers to a comment in which the implicit meaning is different from the explicit meaning, e.g. in IV,8, Antony's 'drink carouses to the next day's fate,/Which promises royal peril' is a toast to his own (rather than to Caesar's) destruction. Also in IV,6, Caesar's comment, 'The time of universal peace is near' is ironic. 'Universal peace' is today no nearer than it has ever been.

metaphor The application of a word or phrase to a concept or object it doesn't literally denote, in order to suggest comparison with another concept or object without using 'like' or 'as'. In V,2 Cleopatra describes Iras as 'an Egyptian puppet' who 'shalt be shown/In Rome, as well as I.' Iras isn't literally a puppet, though she will be treated as one in Rome.

monosyllabic Having only one syllable, as in the word 'yes'. In the final scene of Act IV, Cleopatra's 'Then is it sin/To rush' is monosyllabic.

motif An element, incident, device, word, image or formula which recurs frequently in the play, e.g. the word 'dung' appears in the first scene and in the last scene of the play; the word 'world' is found forty-two times in *Antony and Cleopatra*. A motif entails an implicit theme of the play. Thus *Antony and Cleopatra* is concerned with 'dung' and vanity, with Antony's renunciation of the 'world' for passion.

onomatopoeia A word or group of words whose sound resembles the sound or sense it denotes; e.g. hiss, rumble, murmur, groan.

oxymoron The combining of two terms that are usually contraries, e.g. 'pleasing pains'.

pathos Deep feeling. In *Antony and Cleopatra*, a scene or passage designed to evoke feelings of pity and sorrow from the audience, e.g. Enobarbus's death (IV,9).

pun A play on words (or on a word) that have the same or similar sounds but sharply differ in meaning, e.g. in IV,4 when Antony asks Eros for 'mine armour Eros!' There is a pun on 'armour' which means (a) military uniform (b) passion.

run-on-line(s) Poetic lines in which there is no pause at the end of the poetic line, e.g., Enobarbus's 'throw my heart/Against the flint and hardness of my fault' (IV, 9).

setting The location, historical time and social background in which the action occurs. In *Antony and Cleopatra* the locations are Egypt, Rome, the Eastern Mediterranean; the time 42 BC (three years after the murder of Julius Caesar); 30 BC (the suicides of Antony and Cleopatra). The social background includes the court of Cleopatra, Caesar's home in Rome, Pompey's galley, sentry posts.

simile A comparison between two distinctly different things introduced by 'like' or 'as'.

structure The organization of the play, the way in which the parts relate to the whole. A play can be held together by themes such as conflict, love, war, and relationships (e.g. Antony's relationship with Cleopatra) or contrasts (e.g. Rome and Alexandria). Actions of characters can hold the play together. In *Antony and Cleopatra*, Caesar's actions lead the other characters to make counter-moves. Images can form important links in the structure.

synecdoche Greek for 'taking together' where the part of something is used to signify the whole, e.g. Antony's 'Thou canst not fear us Pompey with thy sails' (II, 6) where 'sails' means ships.

theme Applied to an idea, either implicit or explicit, contained in the play, e.g. private desires as opposed to public duties; Rome and Egypt; hedonism and stoicism.

Note: Students will find the latest edition of M. H. Abrams' *A Glossary of Literary Terms* very useful.

The play

Plot

Following the death of Julius Caesar and the defeat of Brutus and Cassius at the battle of Philippi, the Roman Empire is controlled by three triumvirs, Octavius Caesar, Mark Antony, and Lepidus. Antony, placed in charge of the Eastern provinces, has neglected his administrative duties in order to pursue a passionate love affair in Alexandria with Cleopatra, the Egyptian Queen. Meanwhile the Roman Empire is being torn apart by internal rebellions. Members of Antony's family are involved with a rebellion in Italy, there have been military defeats on the frontiers, the rebel Sextus Pompeius, the son of Pompey the Great, in control of the seas 'hath given the dare to Caesar', and Fulvia, the wife of Antony, has died. These events force Antony to return to Rome.

The triumvirs meet in Rome in order to patch up their differences and to unite against the threat from Pompey. Antony agrees to marry Octavia, the sister of Caesar. The marriage will cement the bond between them. Before fighting, Pompey and the triumvirs decide to talk. They agree upon a peace treaty, and to celebrate Pompey throws a lavish party for them aboard his galley. At the party Lepidus becomes extremely drunk. Caesar and Pompey go to war and Pompey is killed. Caesar, having used Lepidus to defeat Pompey, then gets rid of him. Caesar and Antony now control the Empire. Antony, who is in Athens on political business, sends Octavia to negotiate with her brother on his behalf. However, obsessed with thoughts of Cleopatra, Antony returns to her and to Egypt.

Antony's return to Cleopatra and desertion of Octavia is the signal for the beginning of outright hostilities between him and Caesar. Theirs is a battle for supreme control of the Empire. Cleopatra joins forces with Antony, who has control of the land, but is lured into a naval battle off the coast at Actium. Cleopatra flees from the battle and is followed by Antony. Caesar pursues Antony and Cleopatra to Alexandria. Antony is defeated in battle. He commits suicide after hearing a false report that Cleopatra is dead.

Caesar wants to lead Cleopatra in triumph through the streets of Rome. Cleopatra tricks Caesar; she has an asp brought to her in a fig basket and, with her faithful attendants, commits suicide. Caesar discovers her dead body, and orders that Antony and Cleopatra be buried together and accorded dignified funeral rites.

Sources and treatment

Shakespeare drew upon several sources for Antony and Cleopatra. The chief of these are (1) Sir Thomas North's English version published in 1579 of Amyot's French translation of Plutarch's *Lives of the Noble Grecians and Romans*; (2) Plutarch's *Morals*, translated in 1603; (3) the 1578 translation of Appian's *Roman Civil Wars*. Shakespeare also drew (4) on Chaucer; (5) on Cinthio's Italian tragedy *Cleopatra*, written about 1542, and (6) an Italian life of Cleopatra by Landi written in 1551. Other sources were: (7) Robert Garnier's French play *Marc Antoine* (1578), translated into English by Mary Sidney, Countess of Pembroke (1590); (8) Samuel Daniel's *Tragedy of Cleopatra* (1594, 1599); (9) The Bible: St John's Revelation.

North's translation of Plutarch was used by Shakespeare for his other Roman plays, *Julius Caesar, Coriolanus* and *Timon of Athens*. The main events and incidents of these dramas are in North. *Antony and Cleopatra* is not an exception, and the events recorded by North, and used by Shakespeare, are:

1 Fulvia and Lucius 'jointing their force 'gainst Caesar' (I, 2).

2 The activities of 'Menecrates and Menas, famous pirates' who 'Makes the sea serve them'. Shakespeare makes their activities seem more threatening than does Plutarch (I, 4).

3 The initial meeting between Antony and Cleopatra on the River Cydnus magnificently described by Enobarbus (II, 2).

4 The political agreement suggested by Agrippa, resulting in the marriage between Antony and Octavia (II, 2).

5 Ventidius's activities amongst the Parthians (II, 3; III, 1).

6 The meeting between the triumvirs at Misenum (II, 7), although Shakespeare places greater emphasis than Plutarch upon the potential political conflicts between Pompey, Antony and Caesar.

7 The activities on Pompey's galley (II, 7) and Menas's suggested plot. Plutarch comments that 'Pompey cast anchors enough into the sea to make his galley fast, and then built a bridge of wood to convey them to his galley, from the head of mount Misena: and there he welcomed them, and made them great cheer'. Shakespeare transforms 'great cheer' into a drunken orgy.

8 The battle of Actium, Cleopatra's flight, and Antony's following her (III, 10, 11).
9 Enobarbus's desertion (IV, 6, 9). Plutarch places this before the battle of Actium, Shakespeare after it.
10 The Egyptian battles (IV, 7–8).
11 The death of Antony (IV, 14, 15); Cleopatra's retreat to the monument (IV, 15; V, 2).
12 Caesar's meeting with Cleopatra (V, 2).

North is not merely the foundation for these events but provides the source of various incidents illuminating personality and character. Amongst these are descriptions relating to:
Antony: 'this Herculean Roman' (I,3). In Plutarch he is 'descended from one Anton, the son of Hercules'; respected and popular amongst his soldiers (I,4); Antony's endurance and strength of character following his defeat at Modena (I,4). Then there is his superstitious character (II,3); jealousy of Cleopatra (II,5), especially the fishing incident which Shakespeare transforms into a symbolic representation of Cleopatra and the way she has entrapped him; III,11, when Antony tells Cleopatra 'You did know/How much you were my conqueror'; When Antony orders Thidias to be whipped (III,13); Antony's jealousy of Caesar, for example III,4, where he tells Octavia that her brother 'hath wag'd/New wars 'gainst Pompey', though in this instance Shakespeare departs slightly from Plutarch who notes that Caesar is reading Antony's will rather than his own – Antony tells Octavia that Caesar 'made his will, and read it/To public ear'. Antony's obsession with Cleopatra – Caesar tells Lepidus that Antony 'fishes, drinks, and wastes/The lamps of night in revel' (I,4); Antony's consideration for Julius Caesar and Brutus (III,2).
Cleopatra: her sensuality. Enobarbus's description of her on the river Cydnus (II,2): 'For her own person,/It beggar'd all description: she did lie/In her pavilion – cloth-of-gold, of tissue –/O'erpicturing that Venus where we see/The fancy outwork nature.' This transforms Plutarch's: 'And now for the person of herself: she was layed under a pavilion of cloth of gold of tissue, apparelled and attired like the goddess Venus, commonly drawn in picture'; her vanity, ability to experience extremes of emotion such as love and hate, her tricks, and cowardice – when, for instance, during the battle 'the breeze upon her, like a cow in June,/Hoists sails, and flies' and Antony '(like a doting mallard)/Leaving the fight in height', flies after her' (III,10).
Octavia: her decency, nobility, and patience.
Caesar: his ruthlessness and coldness.

Acts IV and V follow North closely. The Soothsayer's words to Antony, and Antony's recognition of Caesar's better luck at sports (II,3), and the soldier's plea in III,7 that Antony should 'not fight by sea,/Trust not to rotten planks: do you misdoubt/This sword, and these my wounds? Let the Egyptians/And the Phoenicians go a-ducking', almost word for word follow Plutarch. In North a Captain notes 'O noble Emperor, how cometh it to pass that you trust to these vile brittle ships? What, do you mistrust these wounds of mine, and this sword? Let the Egyptians and Phoenicians fight by sea, and set us on the main land.' Yet Shakespeare omits from Plutarch's account Cleopatra's political intrigues and her Athenian visit, Antony's negative Asian campaigns, and the detailed description of the treasure Cleopatra took with her to the monument. Octavia is a personality of considerable stature and authority in Plutarch. Shakespeare reduces her role: his focus is clearly upon Antony and Cleopatra.

Shakespeare expands Plutarch; for example, not present in Plutarch are: the whole of I,2; Cleopatra's dream (V,2); 'I dreamt there was an emperor Antony'; Cleopatra's talk with the clown (V,2); Lepidus's drunken insensibility on Pompey's galley (II,7); Antony's intense anger with Cleopatra (III,13; IV,12); and Cleopatra's questioning of the messenger (II,5, III,3).

Shakespeare drew upon Plutarch's *Morals* (1603) for the comparisons in *Antony and Cleopatra* of Cleopatra with Venus, Ceres, Juno, and with Isis the Moon Goddess. The 1603 translation of Plutarch describes Isis 'as having an infinite number of names, for that she receiveth all forms and shapes, according as it pleaseth that first reason to convert and turn her'. Enobarbus says of Cleopatra that 'Age cannot wither her, not custom stale/Her infinite variety' (II,2).

Appian's *Roman Civil Wars* is the source for Antony's reply to Caesar in II,2 concerning the activities of Lucius, Antony's brother, who rebelled of his own volition against the triumvirate – not on Antony's behalf. Appian is also the source for his comment that Fulvia waged war 'To have me out of Egypt' (II,2). Also (not in Plutarch but in Appian) are Antony's reference to Sextus Pompeius commanding 'the empire of the sea' (I,2), and his comment that the Romans 'began to throw/Pompey the Great, and all his dignities/Upon his son' (I,2). Pompey's death is in Appian, not in Plutarch, and Appian notes that 'There be that say that Plancus, and not Antony, did command him to die', which explains Antony's anger for he 'Threats the throat of that his officer/That murder'd Pompey' (III,5).

For literary handling of the Antony and Cleopatra tragedy Shakespeare had as a model Chaucer's treatment in the *Legend of Good Women* where a highly romanticized Cleopatra is presented, with a discreet hard Antony marrying Cleopatra. There is no Octavia, and insane with despair after defeat at Actium, Antony kills himself. Cinthio's tragedy *Cleopatra* begins after Actium and emphasizes the role of Fortune. Landi's *Life* of Cleopatra is a sympathetic one focusing upon Cleopatra's intelligence.

Robert Garnier's tragedy translated by the Countess of Pembroke, *Marc Antoine*, focuses on Antony, has a moral emphasis and tone, and gives Cleopatra sympathetic consideration: 'She is all heav'nlie'. There are verbal echoes between Garnier's tragedy and Shakespeare's. In the former there is 'fat slime', in Shakespeare 'The higher Nilus swells . . . the slime and ooze scatters' (II,7). In *Antoine* Cleopatra's 'thousand kisses, thousand thousand more' bid Antony farewell. In Shakespeare 'Of many thousand kisses, the poor last' Antony will 'lay upon' Cleopatra's 'lips' (IV,15).

Samuel Daniel's drama *Tragedy of Cleopatra* (1594, 1599), is the foundation for material in *Antony and Cleopatra* not found in other sources. In V,2 Cleopatra reflects on being 'chastis'd with the sober eye/Of dull Octavia'. Daniel also has this detail. Cleopatra's 'wrinkled deep in time' (I,5) echoes Daniel's 'beauties waine', and 'new-appearing wrinkles of declining'. Cleopatra's determination, 'My resolution, and my hands' (IV,15), to commit suicide, Dolabella's love for Cleopatra (V,2), her memory, 'I am again for Cydnus,/To meet Mark Antony' (V,2), and the detail of her crown being 'awry' (V,2), all have their genesis in Daniel. The *Tragedy of Cleopatra* however doesn't emphasize the causes of Antony's fall, though it does place Antony and Cleopatra's tragedy within a universal framework and contrasts Roman austerity with Egyptian luxuriousness. But, perhaps naïvely, it suggests that Antony was ignorant of woman before meeting Cleopatra.

The New Testament Revelation of St John is the foundation for many verbal images and ideas in the play whereas the other sources largely provide the framework for the plotting and its details. There are various instances of Shakespeare's use of Revelation. For instance in the last scene of the play Cleopatra tells Dolabella:

I dreamt there was an Emperor Antony . . .
His face was as the heavens, and therein stuck
A sun and moon, which kept their course, and lighted

The little O, the earth . . .
His legs bestrid the ocean, his rear'd arm
Crested the world: his voice was propertied
As all the tunèd spheres, and that to friends:
But when he meant to quail, and shake the orb,
He was as rattling thunder.

Revelation, X, 1-6 reads:

And I saw another mighty angel come down from heaven, clothed with a cloud . . . and his face was as it were the sun, and his feet as pillars of fire . . . and he set his right foot upon the sea, and his left foot on the earth, and cried with a loud voice . . . and when he had cried, seven thunders uttered their voices . . . And the angel which I saw stand upon these, and the earth, lift up his hand to heaven.

These images of cosmic change, of 'His face . . . as the heavens', of Antony bestriding the universe, and of thunder, are apocalyptic in the sense that they literally anticipate change on a large scale. As in the play the old world of Antony and Cleopatra gives way to Caesar, so in Revelation there is a vision of the end of the world. References to stars, to death, and to the falling of stars permeate Shakespeare's play and the Biblical text. Caesar says that Antony 'hath given his empire/Up to a whore, who now are levying/The Kings o' the earth for war' (III,6). In Revelation, xvii,1–2, there is 'the judgement of the great whore that sitteth upon many waters with whom the kings of the earth have committed fornication'.

In spite of the verbal parallels, the use of plot and character detail, the dependence upon Plutarch and the other sources for basic data, Shakespeare's *Antony and Cleopatra* transcends the raw material of its creation. The play centres upon both Antony and Cleopatra, their middle-aged passion and its tragic consequences. It is enacted against the backcloth of the disintegration of an Empire and conveyed in unique poetry.

Date and text of the play

The play is recorded in the Stationers' Register for 20 May 1608 but appears not to have been published until 1623 as one of the plays in the First Folio (the first collected edition of the plays). Scholarly and critical opinions agree that the play is a relatively late one, having been written probably either in 1606 or 1607. It is a sequel to *Julius Caesar*, which was being performed in London during September 1599. Except for I,1 neither Act nor Scene divisions were indicated in the First Folio. Those in modern texts largely follow the divisions into Acts and Scenes made by Nicholas Rowe (1674–1718). The text we are reading contains materials introduced by editors after 1623. Thus, to cite one instance, at the end of Act I, Cleopatra's 'My salad days,/ When I was green in judgment, cold in blood' contain additions by the 18th-century scholar Warburton who added the words 'green in judgment, cold in blood'.

Scene summaries, critical commentary, textual notes and revision questions

Act I Scene 1

The play opens in Cleopatra's Alexandria Palace. Two friends of Mark Antony, Philo and Demetrius, discuss Cleopatra's power over Antony. Instead of being a ruler he is ruled, and gives up his responsibilities for love. The grand entrance of Antony and Cleopatra serves to emphasize Philo's observations. A messenger with news from Rome is ignored; totally absorbed in each other, Antony and Cleopatra exchange views on love and faithfulness. Alone again, Demetrius and Philo observe that what they have witnessed confirms that Antony is not his former self.

Commentary

This brief scene of sixty-two lines presents themes, characters, and concerns to be treated throughout the play. The opening speech contains different attitudes to Antony's relationship with Cleopatra; on the one hand grand passion and infatuation are conveyed in the word 'dotage', on the other hand victimization and disapproval – a great Roman General 'is become the bellows and the fan/To cool a gipsy's lust'.

The play starts in the middle of a speech with 'Nay but'; Shakespeare is probably using this as a device to gain his audience's attention, which the entrance of Antony and Cleopatra immediately focuses upon them. Their appearance emphasizes visual aspects present throughout, and contrasts the sombrely dressed Romans in their plate and armour with the voluptuous 'tawny' Egyptians. The contrast between Rome and Egypt, the conflict between Cleopatra and Antony, and Antony's internal psychological struggle between duty and passion, are central preoccupations of *Antony and Cleopatra*.

Other important elements in the opening scene are the introduction of Antony and Cleopatra, the nature of her relationship with Antony and Antony's attitudes. Cleopatra is both dominant and sceptical. 'If it be love indeed,' she taunts Antony, 'tell me how much.' Antony, 'the triple pillar of the world' is 'transform'd/Into a strumpet's fool'. Antony is prepared to renounce all for love – 'The nobleness of life/Is to do thus'.

Also in this scene there is a taste of the powerful evocative imagery pervading the play. Antony wants 'the wide arch/of the rang'd empire' to 'fall' so that he can love. The world, the Roman Empire, can disintegrate so that Antony and Cleopatra can enjoy love. Antony tells Cleopatra: 'There's not a minute of our lives should stretch/Without some pleasure now.' All is to be reduced and sacrificed for the sensual pleasure of the moment – hedonism (the pleasure principle) is to predominate over duty and responsibility.

dotage Infatuation, 'doting on' someone.
O'erflows the measure Goes beyond the limit. The metaphor is from a liquid overflowing from the measuring cup.
those his i.e. in the past, in contrast to 'this dotage' of the present.
　goodly Several meanings (a) worthwhile, (b) implication of 'godly', like the Gods.
files and musters The army lined up for formal inspection.
plated Armoured, an early instance of the war metaphors pervading the play.
　Mars The Roman God of War.
　bend Incline, bending over.
office and devotion His duties and his desires have been the same.
tawny front Brown face. Note the pun on 'front': The 'front line of battle' and 'face'.
　captain's i.e. commander's.
reneges all temper Forgets discipline and self-control.
fan (a) to cool the fire down. Note the antithesis 'bellows'–'fan'. The implication is that Antony has become an object, a victim to be heated up and cooled down.
gipsy's (a) Egyptian's (b) whore's.
Eunuchs Sexless.
triple pillar One of the three Triumvirs (council of three) ruling the Roman Empire after Caesar's assassination. The other two were Octavius Caesar, who controlled the Western Empire, with Lepidus controlling Italy. Antony controlled the Eastern Empire.
strumpet Prostitute.
　fool Toy, plaything.
beggary in the love . . . reckoned The love that can exactly be calculated is a poor love.
bourn Limit.
Then must . . . earth The limit of my love reaches beyond the heaven and the earth. cf. Revelation, xxi,1: 'And I saw a new heaven and a new earth'.
News . . . from Rome Notice that Rome belongs to the Old World.
Grates me, the sum This gets on my nerves, tell me the essence of it.
Fulvia Antony's wife.

scarce-bearded Caesar The young Caesar, Octavius Caesar, who was
about twenty-three, Antony being about twenty years older.

Take in Conquer.

 enfranchise Liberate.

dismission Dismissal.

process Summons to appear at the Law Courts.

homager Vassal.

else so Why else.

 thy cheek . . . scolds Why are you blushing when your wife calls?

Tiber The main river of Rome.

melt . . . fall Powerful images of disintegration which pervade the play.

 rang'd empire Spread out.

Here Where Cleopatra is.

clay Subject to decay and erosion.

 dungy As dung, worthless.

the nobleness of life . . . up peerless What is noble in life consists in
our mutual love and I command the rest of the world to acknowledge
our love.

Excellent falsehood Oxymoron. Cleopatra casts scorn on Antony's
noble values.

stirr'd (a) impassioned (b) influenced.

confound Waste.

conference Conversation.

approves the common liar Proves correct the rumours.

Act I Scene 2

After some talk between a Soothsayer and Enobarbus and the
queen's attendants in which Charmian's and Iras's fortunes are
told, Cleopatra comes in search of Antony. She has remembered
the messenger from Rome and has gone to find him. The
messenger brings news of chaos in Italy and military defeats in
Syria and Asia. Another messenger has brought news of the
death of Fulvia, Antony's wife. Antony becomes aware of his
responsibilities and realizes that he must depart at once from
Cleopatra and Egypt. Enobarbus, not fully comprehending that
Fulvia is dead, or being sure how Antony will take the news, jests
with him and comments on Cleopatra's passion for him. Antony
tells Enobarbus the seriousness of the political situation, of the
disintegration of the Roman Empire, and of the urgent necessity
for him (Antony) to return home.

Commentary

The scene introduces Cleopatra's friends, and Antony's loyal lieutenant Enobarbus. The initial dialogue is representative of the bawdiness of the play, while the Soothsayer's predictions provide an ironic commentary on what is to happen: their 'former fortune' is 'fairer' than 'that which is to approach'. The Soothsayer injects a serious element into the proceedings. Although Enobarbus says very little, and enjoys drinking and jesting, his actions and comments also introduce a sombre element into the hedonistic atmosphere. He admits that his 'and most of our fortunes tonight, shall be – drunk to bed' and jests with Antony about 'death'.

Cleopatra's insight is shown during her brief appearance. She is preoccupied with finding her 'lord' Antony, yet she is aware of his other obligations and that 'A Roman thought has struck him'. And she is prepared to play games with him; she departs when she hears he is approaching. Antony's reactions to the public events of the rebellions in the Empire, and to private tragedies such as his wife's death, reveal that he is a soldier, administrator, man of responsibility and action. His view of events and duty is Roman rather than the Egyptian pleasure-seeking outlook.

The opening use of prose with its bawdy innuendoes contrasts with the subsequent use of poetry in the scene, reflecting a change of mood and values from the enjoyment of the moment to serious issues of order and government. Metaphors convey the conflict Antony experiences. He compares himself with a weedy field: 'we bring forth weeds,/When our quick minds lie still.' On the other hand he is aware that 'these strong Egyptian fetters I must break,/Or lose myself in dotage.' Names of rebels such as Labienus and of places such as Lydia and Ionia serve to place Antony and Cleopatra in perspective. They are not isolated; Egypt also is part of a larger world.

O that I ... garlands Two meanings: (a) Charmian's husband will go up to the altar innocently to get married unaware that she already has a lover and he has been cuckolded; (b) her husband will be a champion cuckold and receive a garland for being so.

I make not i.e. I'm not inventing this.

one i.e. a piece of good fortune.

fairer (a) more beautiful (b) nobler – in her loyalty, anticipating subsequent dramatic action, Cleopatra in V,2 calls her 'noble'.

shall paint Put on make-up.

prescience Intuition.

more beloving ... belov'd i.e. (a) you will love Cleopatra more than she loves you, or (b) you will love your suitors more than they will love you.

heat . . . drinking Elizabethans thought that love and wine both heated the liver which was regarded as the seat of the affections.

Herod of Jewry Upon hearing of Jesus's birth, King Herod is said to have put to the sword many of the first-born of Israel.

Find me i.e. read my hand – palmistry.

companion me with my mistress i.e. as the wife of a triumvir, she would then be equal in rank with her mistress Cleopatra.

prov'd Experienced.

have no names Be illegitimate.

fertile A pun on (a) fertility (b) foretelling.

forgive thee for a witch You are a wizard so I'll forgive you.

palm presages chastity Iras is probably looking at the palm of her own hand.

Nilus Ironic – the Nile, the main river in Egypt, overflows its banks frequently and creates a fertile strip in the Egyptian desert.

oily palm Charmian now refers to Iras's palm.

scratch mine ear i.e. do the simplest thing.

mend Check, correct.

cannot go Is unable to produce children.

Isis Egyptian goddess of fertility, the moon, and justice.

cuckold A man whose wife has been sexually unfaithful to him.

loose-wiv'd Married to a woman of loose morals.

foul Ugly.

uncuckolded Not betrayed by his wife.

keep decorum . . . accordingly i.e. act as you think fit, and as a Goddess.

A Roman thought (a) A thought of Rome (b) A reflection upon duty rather than love.

Fulvia . . . field Fulvia took up arms, another example of a powerful woman.

better issue Success.

infects the teller i.e. makes him seem bad too.

as he As if he.

Labienus . . . Ionia North's Plutarch notes 'Labienus conquered all Asia with the armie of the Parthians' . . . Labienus had been a Roman general and defected. His activities are in contrast to Antony's inactivity.

Euphrates The river flowing from Eastern Turkey through Syria and Iraq and finishing near the Persian Gulf.

Lydia An area west of Asia Minor.

Ionia Also western Asia Minor.

thou Note that 'thou' was used by a master or mistress to servants, close friends or as a term of affectionate endearment.

home Honestly and to the point.

O then we bring . . . i.e. having bad things spelled out to us is as good as ploughing a weedy field.

earing Ploughing.

Sicyon Greek city near Corinth.

What are you? The messenger doesn't answer the question but blurts out the news.

Importeth It is important for.

Forbear Put up with me.

Thus . . . desire it i.e. I wanted it to happen.

By revolution lowering The more we have of something the less we desire it.

could Would like to.

shov'd her on i.e. towards her death.

enchanting queen Cleopatra, whose spell he is under.

idleness i.e. time spent with Cleopatra.

death's . . . word A pun: 'to die' here probably means to experience sexual orgasm.

between them . . . nothing Matters of state and politics should come before women's concerns.

I have seen her . . . moment She has been sexually stimulated by far less important events.

mettle Strength.

celerity Quickness.

She is . . . thought i.e. she is crafty, with the suggestion of play-acting. Also there is the suggestion that she is more skilful than men.

winds and waters Changing moods.

almanacs Methods of predicting the weather, storms, tempests and other dangers to shipping.

if it be i.e. the opposite – playing games.

Jove The king of the gods, and the Roman god of rain.

left unseen . . . your travel i.e. you'd have missed experiencing and enjoying one of the wonders of the world.

Fulvia is dead Note the repetitions and literal matter-of-factness of Antony's comment. He is in no mood, at the moment, to jest with Enobarbus.

the tailors of the earth i.e. the basic realities of living.

when old robes . . . new i.e. when old wives die new wives may be found.

a cut A pun (a) a loss (b) the style of clothing.

crown'd with consolation i.e. something good will come of it.

old smock i.e. Fulvia.

new petticoat i.e. Cleopatra.

the tears live . . . this sorrow i.e. the tears shed for Fulvia could also be caused by an onion.

your abode Your staying here.

our Note that Antony removes himself from Enobarbus's familiarity by the use of the royal 'our'.

break Make known, i.e. 'break the news'.

expedience Immediate departure.

her leave to part Her permission to depart.

us Antony uses the royal plural. He has reassumed his commander's role.

contriving Plotting on our side.

Sextus Pompeius Younger son by Pompey the Great. After Julius Caesar's death he was in charge of the Roman navy. He gained command of the sea, attacked Italy, and subjected its ports to blockade.

dare Defeat.

slippery Changeable, unreliable.

Pompey the Great The great Roman general, 106–48 BC, and Julius Caesar's rival. Caesar defeated him in Greece. Pompey sought refuge in Egypt, where he was murdered. Perhaps Antony is also here thinking of his own possible fate.

blood and life Energy, courage and actuality.

stands up . . . main soldier Sets himself up as the greatest soldier in the world.

whose quality . . . danger By his nature (personality) if allowed to continue, may well destroy the unity of the Roman Empire like the courser's hair. A reference to the superstition that horse hair dropped into water is transformed into worms or eels.

A serpent's poison i.e. this horse hair become a 'living creature' can turn into a serpent.

Say our pleasure . . . hence i.e. tell whomever it is necessary to inform, that we are leaving immediately.

Act I Scene 3

Cleopatra sends one of her attendants to search for Antony, with instructions that if he finds Antony happy he must say that Cleopatra is sad, and vice versa. Charmian disagrees with Cleopatra's strategy for keeping Antony with her. When Antony appears, Cleopatra continuously interrupts him and varies in her attitude and mood towards him. He tells her that he is to leave Egypt and that his wife Fulvia has died. Cleopatra's mood changes to a serious one and she finds it difficult to express her feelings.

Commentary

There are five main areas of interest in this fascinating scene: Cleopatra's emotional manipulation of Antony and the changes in her attitude towards him and the situation in which she finds herself; Antony's mixed emotional attitude to Cleopatra; the way in which the play's theme of public duty versus private desires and passions is conveyed; the way in which political events and activities reflect and parallel private ones; and the final speeches in the Act, in which love seems to become greater than mutable events or private desires.

Cleopatra's manipulation of Antony may be seen in her initial games playing, and her instructions to Charmian and Alexas; her pretending to be 'sick and sullen' as soon as Antony appears, in order to arouse his sympathies; from his eyes she knows 'there's some good news'. She taunts him that his attitude to 'the married woman' is the reason he is leaving her. She questions his continuing fidelity to her since he has been false to Fulvia, either she or Antony are still in love, she continues, or else Antony 'the greatest soldier of the world,/Art turn'd the greatest liar'. Uncertain of Antony's actual emotional reaction to Fulvia's death, she provokes him but at the end of the scene she accepts his call to 'honour' and hopes that 'all the gods go with' him.

Antony's attitude to Cleopatra is one of mixed emotions. In terms of stage presence he plays a lesser role to that of Cleopatra. He is forced to speak in half comments 'Now, my dearest queen—' 'The gods best know—' while she speaks on. His speeches, when he is allowed to make them, place emphasis upon his responsibilities as a ruler, upon disorder in the Roman Empire, and exhibit a return to the Roman values of 'honour' and duty. His final words reflect his deep love for Cleopatra – 'I, hence fleeting, here remain with thee'. The conflict between private passions, desires and inclinations and public duty is conveyed in the conflict between Antony and Cleopatra, and Antony's own internal struggle as he is forced by external events beyond his control to leave his passionately loved Cleopatra.

I ... you i.e. tell him this, I didn't send you.
hold the method Use the right tactics.
breathing Expression.
the sides of nature ... sustain it The body won't put up with it.
married woman Fulvia; Cleopatra refuses to speak her name.
yet at ... planted I knew from the very start of our relationship that you were playing games.
planted (a) like seeds (b) like mines as in warfare i.e. between Antony and Cleopatra.
Which ... swearing Which are broken the moment they are spoken.
colour Excuse.
Eternity ... eyes Great poetry; notice the contrast within the seven-word line between the duosyllabic 'Eternity' placed at the beginning of the line and the subsequent monosyllables, and the use of 'was' – the emotion was in the past; Cleopatra uses the royal 'our', referring to them both.

brows' bent i.e. the bend or arch of our eyebrows, which by implication are contrasted to the arch of a rainbow or heaven. Note the alliterative 'b' sounds=strength of love.

none . . . heaven Even the humblest parts of our bodies were endowed with the divine image.

  race Sprung from, as high as.

in Egypt i.e. in the country and in herself, Cleopatra.

strong . . . time Ironic, contrasted with Cleopatra's 'eternity'.

  strong Urgent.

Our . . . my The pronouns distinguish Antony's duty as a ruler and his behaviour as a lover.

full heart . . . with you i.e. remains with you.

Shines . . . swords i.e. is experiencing Civil War.

Equality . . . faction The equal strength of two powers which are uncertain of the future and unable to trust one another, leads to separate factions arising.

  faction A conspiracy, a separate group.

And quietness . . . change i.e. it has been too peaceful at home for too long, sickness has resulted and will only be cured by the blood-letting of war. (It was believed that diseases were cured by bleeding.)

safe Safeguard.

Though age from . . . childishness My age does not stop me from being deceived by you, but it does prevent me from childish stupidity in believing everything I'm told.

Can Fulvia die? i.e. is it really true that she is dead?

garboils Troubles, disturbances of a civil, political nature.

last i.e. end of the letter.

the sacred vials . . . water A reference to the Roman custom of placing bottles of tears in friends' tombs.

which . . . advice Which exist or stop according to your commands.

the fire . . . slime i.e. the heat of the sun was supposed to generate life from the mud of the Nile.

Cut my lace Loosen my tight bodice; give me air.

An honourable trial i.e. separation.

So . . . told me i.e. Cleopatra doesn't believe him.

Belong to Egypt i.e. are for Cleopatra as Egyptian Queen.

play one scene . . . excellent dissembling i.e. perform a little first-class acting.

perfect honour Contrasts with 'excellent dissembling' and echoes Antony's 'honourable trial' and 'true evidence'.

meetly Not bad.

Herculean Hercules in Roman mythology represented physical strength. Antony, according to North's Plutarch, prided himself on being descended from Hercules. The Globe Theatre, where Shakespeare's plays were performed, had as its sign a picture of Hercules carrying a globe.

become/The carriage of his chafe How gracefully Hercules's
descendant acts out his anger.

Sir, you . . . not it Note her suggestive and alluring repetitions
reminding him of their past love for each other.

But that your . . . your subject If you didn't rule over idleness.

Eye well to you Attract you.

laurel victory The Roman laurel wreath signified victory.

strewed A reference to the custom of throwing flowers before a
successful general.

Our separation . . . thee Cleopatra stays in Egypt, Antony departs, yet
their spirits and thoughts remain together though physically they are
separated. (In *The Phoenix and the Turtle* Shakespeare writes of 'Hearts
remote, yet not asunder'.)

Act I Scene 4

In his house in Rome Octavius Caesar reads a letter from
Alexandria outlining Antony's activities. Caesar comments on
these to Lepidus, who tries in vain to defend Antony from
Caesar's accusations. A messenger arrives with news that Pompey, a major threat to the leadership of the Roman Empire, has
gained strength at sea. Octavius Caesar contrasts Antony's
'lascivious wassails' with his previous heroic behaviour and hopes
that 'his shames' will 'quickly/Drive him to Rome'. He and Lepidus must gather together what armed forces they can in order
to defend Pompey and his forces.

Commentary

Among several interesting elements at work are the change in
scene and action from Alexandria and Cleopatra's palace to
Rome and to Octavius Caesar's home. The transfer from one
seat of power to another reflects different value systems and
attitudes to life. Both centres of power are united, although for
different reasons, in wanting Antony. Octavius Caesar, a representative of Roman values, casts scorn upon Antony's Alexandrian activities, in which he has given up 'a kingdom for a mirth,
to sit/And keep the turn of tippling with a slave,' also 'To reel the
streets at noon, and stand the buffet/With knaves that smells of
sweat'.

Alexandrian hedonism is contrasted with Roman austerity.
We are introduced to Antony's fellow triumvirs. Lepidus says
little, thus reflecting his place in the ruling triumvirate. Octavius

Caesar exhibits shrewdness and calculation, assessing fairly Antony's strengths and weaknesses. His account of Antony's heroism after his defeat at Modena shows a side of Antony not yet encountered in the play, and demonstrates the way in which Shakespeare uses and transcends his source materials.

In addition to an assertion of Roman values of duty, heroism, and abstinence, an introduction to Octavius and Lepidus, and giving another view of Antony's character, the scene also continues the theme of internal disruption and chaos that pervades the play. The passion of Antony and Cleopatra is played out against the backdrop of a disintegrating Empire, a power struggle, and Machiavellian intrigue.

competitor Colleague, i.e. Antony.

queen of Ptolemy i.e. Cleopatra. Under the terms of her father's will and according to custom she married Ptolemy, her eldest brother. He refused to share power with her, and exiled her. Julius Caesar restored her to the throne, and Ptolemy drowned. She then, at Caesar's command, married her younger brother (also a Ptolemy) whom, it is said, she poisoned.

hardly gave audience i.e. to Caesar's messengers mentioned in I,1 and seen by Antony in I,2.

A man ... follow A man who is the representative of all human vices.
  abstract Sum total, representative.

spots of heaven i.e. the stars.

by Contrasted with.

purchas'd Learned, acquired.

turn of tippling Drinking bouts.

stand the buffet Exchange blows (as in wrestling, or in boxing).

composure Personality, temperament.

foils (a) actions (b) echo of 'faults' (c) errors.

we do bear ... lightness i.e. when his irresponsible actions place an additional burden on his colleagues (fellow triumvirs).

vacancy Leisure time.

surfeits i.e. too much of various things.

dryness of his bones His bones will dry up.

for't To answer for it.

but to ... sport ... and ours He is wasting time on his own pleasure which should be spent on matters of state. Note the use of the metaphor from warfare, a soldier being summoned to parade by the drum.

As we rate ... pleasure i.e. we tell off boys who are old enough to know better not to waste time. Similarly we expect men to act their age.

Pawn i.e. (a) exchange (b) allow reason to be replaced by emotion.

to judgment i.e. against mature judgement or opinion.

primal state First governments.

he which is . . . were He who is now in power wishes that he were in the position he was before coming to power, i.e. popular.

the ebb'd man The man whose fortunes are against him.

Comes dear'd . . . lack'd Is valued when absent.

vagabond flag . . . tide Reed moving aimlessly on the water.

lackeying i.e. like a servant running after his master.

To rot . . . motion The reeds and iris rot themselves on the water; the mob destroys itself through its unrest and discontent.

Menecrates and Menas North's Plutarch: 'two notable pirates, Menas, and Menecrates . . . so scored all the sea . . . that none durst peep out with a sail'.

hot inroads Fierce track.

Lack blood . . . on't Become white at the thought of it.

flush Hot-blooded.

strikes more . . . resisted His name is more powerful than resisting him in battle would be.

wassails Revels.

Modena About 112 km (70 m) NNW of Florence in Italy. Antony was defeated there by the consuls Hirtius and Pansa. In his escape he suffered great hardships.

whom i.e. famine.

patience Endurance.

stale Urine.

gilded puddle Urine yellowed with filth.

deign Not reject.

rudest Wildest.

lank'd not Did not grow thin.

I can be able . . . time I shall be able to deal with this immediate crisis.

encounter Meeting, conference.

stirs Events.

I knew . . . bond I am aware it is my duty.

Act I Scene 5

Cleopatra's obsession with Antony runs riot in his absence. She sends constant messages to him, indulges in fantasies, comparing him with some of her past lovers, and especially with Julius Caesar, whom she loved when she 'was green in judgment'.

Commentary

The emphasis in this scene is upon the imagination. It is full of bawdy innuendo suggesting the intensity of Cleopatra's passion for Antony and how her need for him increases in his absence. The past is contrasted with the present, Cleopatra's past lovers with her present isolation. Notice that her lovers have been powerful political figures – rulers. A suggestion of Cleopatra's power and influence over men is conveyed for instance in her bawdy description of 'great Pompey' who 'would stand and make his eyes grow in my brow,/There would he anchor his aspect, and die/ With looking on his life.'

Cleopatra's banter with the eunuch Mardian, her comment to him 'I take no pleasure/In aught an eunuch has', serves to emphasize her essential sexuality. Without sexual expression Cleopatra is unable to live. This is conveyed in her magnificent poetic lines following Charmian's asking her why she requires mandragora to drink. Cleopatra answers: 'That I might sleep out this great gap of time/My Antony is away.' While he is away from her she is only partially alive.

Cleopatra and the absent Antony are the focus of the scene. Her flight of fantasy, her sense of boredom and isolation without Antony, provide an immediate contrast with the previous scene. This was set in another world, with an emphasis upon facts, everyday realities, and a deprecation of sexual indulgence. Alexandria and Rome are two different worlds, linked by Antony.

mandragora A plant with strong narcotic properties; an aphrodisiac.
'tis treason i.e. to say that I think too much of him.
eunuch A castrated male.
unseminar'd A eunuch.
freer Innocent; less restricted or confined.
Indeed A pun: both exclamation of surprise and 'in action'.
Venus did with Mars Venus (Goddess of Love) became the lover of Mars (God of War).
he i.e. Antony.
Do bravely Carry yourself with pride.
wot'st Do you know.
mov'st Carry.
demi-Atlas In mythology Atlas supported the heavens on his shoulders. In Cleopatra's fantasies Antony supports half of the earth. Also a reference to the two worlds – Rome and Egypt.
burgonet Protector worn by horsemen.
Now . . . poison i.e. now I revel in enjoyable fantasies.
Phoebus' The Greek sun god's.
Broad-fronted Bald. The reference is to Julius Caesar, whose mistress Cleopatra had been when she was young.
morsel i.e. a very attractive woman.
great Pompey Historically, Pompey's son became Cleopatra's lover. The reference may also be to Julius Caesar's great rival, Pompey the father.

anchor Rest.

on his life i.e. at Cleopatra.

great med'cine Elixir of life, the agent renewing youth and vitality. It changed base metals into gold.

his tinct His influence, his transforming, life-giving spirit.

 gilded thee Infused thee: i.e. base metal has been transformed.

brave Fine, distinguished.

orient Bright, eastern.

pearl The emblem of truth and fidelity.

mend Improve.

 piece Add to.

mount Climb on, leap on a horse.

arm-gaunt steed Battle worn.

beastly dumb'd Silenced by the beast.

well-divided disposition! Well-balanced. Cleopatra is being ironic at Antony's expense. He is not 'well-balanced'.

'tis the man i.e. that is exactly Antony.

The violence of . . . else i.e. the passion between them is beyond comparison.

posts Messengers.

several Separate.

so thick i.e. in quick succession.

Caesar i.e. her ex-lover Julius Caesar.

Be chok'd . . . emphasis i.e. you deserve to choke.

paragon i.e. compare.

I sing but after you i.e. I am only doing what you did.

green in judgment Innocent, immature.

unpeople Egypt i.e. by sending everyone to Antony as messengers.

Revision questions on Act I

1 Explain the dramatic significance of the first scene of the play.

2 By the end of the first Act what do you think the attitude to Antony is of (a) Cleopatra (b) Octavius Caesar?

3 Illustrate the ways in which the Act reflects Antony's 'well-divided disposition'.

4 Discuss the significance of the news of Fulvia's death.

5 Compare and contrast Cleopatra's behaviour before and after Antony's departure for Rome.

Act II Scene 1

At Pompey's house in Messina Pompey discusses the current situation with the pirates Menas and Menecrates. The main threat to Pompey comes from the experienced soldier Antony, who is languishing in Egypt. Varrius, Pompey's ally, arrives with the unwelcome news that Antony has left Egypt, returned to Rome and joined with Pompey's enemies, the other Triumvirs Caesar and Lepidus. Menas tries to reassure Pompey by reminding him of the enmity between Caesar and Antony concerning the conflict started by Fulvia – Antony's wife. The realist Pompey deduces that internal differences will be papered over in order to combat any external threat.

Commentary

This brief scene of 52 lines is not without significance, drawing attention as it does to the fact that the play deals with power struggles and human conflict for political control. The scene conveys some of the historical background to the events of the play and the extent of the external and internal threats to the Roman Empire. Pompey is motivated not merely by personal ambition but by revenge. Octavius Caesar's uncle and adopted father Julius Caesar had gained the Empire from Pompey's father. On the other hand, the scene shows Pompey's allies Menecrates and Menas as natural rebels against existing power structures.

Notice the contrast in setting, atmosphere and characters with the previous scene. Cleopatra's palace, sexual frustration, desire and Egypt, are replaced by Roman political squabbling. The scene also contains opinions of Antony from others. Indeed the poetic imagery of the scene is conveyed through thoughts of Cleopatra's 'wan'd lip', Antony's 'brain fuming' whilst 'Epicurean cooks/Sharpen with cloyless sauce his appetite'. Note Pompey's observations on the other triumvirs. He has insight into, for instance, Lepidus's cunning. Lepidus flatters both Caesar and Antony, 'Of both is flatter'd: but he neither loves,/Nor either cares for him.'

suitors Pleaders.
  decays Loses the value of.
ourselves i.e. what is in our best interests.
Beg often our own harms i.e. 'ask for trouble'.
we profit . . . prayers Notice the use of alliterative 'p' and 'o' sounds in order to emphasize the antithesis between profit and loss.
me . . . mine The repetitions of the personal pronouns draw attention to Pompey's egoism.
crescent Growing (i.e. as the moon – the imagery is extended in the following lines).
auguring Prophesying.

it . . . full My powers, which are similar to the crescent moon, will grow into full vigour.

without doors i.e. outside Egypt. He'll make wars of love indoors.

Are in the field Ready for battle.

charms Spells.

wan'd The meaning has been the subject of debate. It could refer to the withered moon: in that sense the meaning runs 'Cleopatra is like the moon which wanes past her peak'. N. F. Blake in his *Shakespeare's Language* (1983) suggests that 'wand' rather than 'wan'd' should be used; it 'could refer to a magic wand as used by sorcerers'. If so; 'charmes – wand – Witchcraft decorate a single idea through the choice of related words . . . Cleopatra might well have lips that charm, for in the next line witchcraft is said to team up with beauty.'

brain fuming It was thought that alcohol rose to the brain and fuddled it.

Epicurean cooks i.e. cooks whose exotic dishes satisfy Antony's gluttony. Epicurus was a fourth-century BC Greek philosopher. His teachings were (probably mistakenly) interpreted as recommending hedonism, a life of sensual pleasure, as the way to lead a full life.

cloyless sauce i.e. a sauce of which one never grows tired.

prorogue . . . dullness i.e. his honour will not be operating and there will come a time when he'll totally forget honour. In classical mythology Lethe was one of the rivers of Hades (Hell, the underworld) from which the dead drank and totally forgot their past life.

prorogue Prevent the operation of.

A space for farther travel There has been enough time for an even longer journey.

I could . . . ear I should have heard less important news with greater pleasure.

our opinion i.e. of ourselves (not Antony).

stirring Action.

well gree Get on well.

His wife that's . . . upon him Lucius Antonius joined Fulvia's campaign against Caesar.

mov'd Encouraged.

lesser enmities . . . greater i.e. they may patch up their differences because of our opposition.

pregnant Expected.

 square Quarrelled.

entertained Received.

It only stands . . . upon i.e. it's only a matter of life and death to us.

Act II Scene 2

This scene set in Lepidus's house is divided into two sections: the first is dominated by political considerations, the second by

Enobarbus's evocative description of Cleopatra. The triumvirs meet to thrash out their differences and to try to settle old scores amicably. Caesar and Antony with difficulty refrain from open hostility. Agrippa suggests that Antony should marry Caesar's sister and thereby cement the bonds between the two. Antony and Caesar agree, shake hands, swear to act as brothers, and plan to defeat Pompey.

After Antony and Caesar have gone to see Octavia to get her approval, Enobarbus, Agrippa and Maecenas remain on stage. The theme of their conversation is Cleopatra, her personality and power over Antony.

Commentary

This lengthy scene has three focal points of interest: the conflict between Antony and Caesar; the arranged marriage between Octavia and Antony; and Enobarbus's description of Cleopatra.

The opening conversation between Enobarbus and Lepidus sets the scene for the ensuing confrontation. Lepidus says that public considerations should come before private ones: ''Tis not a time/For private stomaching'. Enobarbus is aware of the depth of personal feeling between Antony and Caesar. These two engage in a lengthy political fencing match which often fails to conceal the depth of personal antagonism between them. Notice Antony's restraint and seeming willingness to 'patch a quarrel' and his defence of his honesty and honour. Differing viewpoints on what has happened in the Empire are given, including Antony's blaming Fulvia, his late wife. 'Truth is, that Fulvia,/To have me out of Egypt, made wars here'. Notice that prose is assigned to Enobarbus's cynical but all too direct objections which are quickly shut up by Antony. For Enobarbus the conflict between Antony and Caesar is fundamentally a personal one, and they 'shall have time to wrangle in, when [they] have nothing else to do'.

The consummate politician Agrippa, Caesar's friend, suggests a brilliant compromise, a marriage of convenience. The opening fencing match between Antony and Octavius prepares the ground for this piece of sordid political manipulation. The construction leading up to Agrippa's suggestion is prepared like moves in a chess game. The battle begins with Caesar's 'frigid' words 'Welcome to Rome', Antony's cool 'Thank you', and 'Sit', with Caesar's suspicious 'Sit, sir'. Antony, having shifted the blame on to Fulvia, is now prepared to come to terms. There is irony in Antony's comment, 'I am not married, Caesar', when we know his thoughts are dominated by Cleopatra. Antony here seems degraded, and he lacks honour yet faces squarely the political problems, regrets the treatment of Caesar's ambassadors and credibly shows that Fulvia's role shouldn't be ignored. Octavius on the other hand expresses love for his sister Octavia, yet sacrifices her on the altar of political expediency.

Enobarbus's account of Cleopatra, with its emphasis upon her sensuality provide a further example of the Roman—Egyptian contrast reverberating throughout the drama. Egyptian love is passionate and doesn't need the sanctification of marriage, whereas Roman 'love' is without emotional substance. Arranged political marriages seem to be the order of the day.

move Annoy.

look over Caesar's head i.e. treat him as an inferior person.

as loud As forcefully.

Jupiter King of the Roman gods who in paintings and sculpture was depicted with a strong growth of beard.

Were I . . . today To pluck a person's beard was regarded as a great insult and the cause for a quarrel. Enobarbus is challenging Lepidus. There is also an allusion to the 'scarce-bearded' Caesar who contrasts with the virile Antony.

private stomaching Personal feuds.

compose Reach an agreement.

leaner Insignificant.

When we debate . . . wounds When we fiercely argue over minor matters we destroy what we are trying to mend.

Touch Refer to.

Nor curstness . . . matter i.e. let us not become embittered.

Sit . . . then One tries to vie with the other in being polite. Antony and Caesar are ill at ease with each other.

Or being i.e. being ill.

concern you not i.e. they are to do with Antony's personal affairs.

with you . . . world With you of all people in the world.

practise on my state Intrigue against my authority.

question Concern.

theme Of concern.

 word of war (a) i.e. they used your name (b) you were the cause of the conflict. Note the triple alliteration 'were', 'word', 'war', and that Caesar refers to the past.

You do mistake Antony refers to the present rather than to the past.

Did urge me Used my name.

stomach Desire.

patch Create.

If you'll . . . this i.e. if you wish to create a quarrel you'll have to find more substantial reasons than these.

I am certain. . .thought I am certain that you were sure to think.

with graceful eyes attend Look favourably on.

As for my wife . . . another i.e. as for Fulvia I wish you were also married to a wife of such spirit.

snaffle An easy bridle-bit for a fast horse. Ironic; Antony is prepared to give up a 'third o' th' world' and 'with a snaffle' to remain with Cleopatra.

not wanted. . . policy too Were not without political cunning.

I grieving grant Did . . . disquiet I admit with regret that I caused you concern.

missive Messenger.

of audience Your presence.

did want of what . . . morning Was not the same man as in the morning. A euphuism (an elaborate way of saying that he was drunk).

Supposing that . . . lack'd it Assuming that I had lost my honour.

poisoned hours i.e. time spent with Cleopatra. Antony uses 'poisoned' with its suggestions of drugged, and of Cleopatra being a poisoner; also notice 'hours' – the play is full of references to time.

it i.e. honesty and reputation.

motive Cause.

noble Nobly and with dignity; honestly.

griefs Grievances.

return it i.e. to the quarrel. Enobarbus is again exhibiting cynical realism – he knows that they cannot remain friends for long.

presence Distinguished company.

your considerate stone i.e. I'll remain silent (yet aware).

conditions Personalities.

hoop The metal band holding barrel staves together; to bind together – as does a wedding ring.

  staunch Strong, firm.

by the mother's side i.e. half-sister.

your reproof . . . rashness She'd justly tell you off.

import Carry with them.

truths would . . . be truths True accounts of your quarrels would be treated as stories, whereas now only half truths are believed to be true.

By duty ruminated A product of a sense of duty.

unto Over.

May I never . . . impediment i.e. in the sense of a barrier or obstacle between minds.

thy hand Notice that Antony addresses Caesar in the informal second person singular, whereas Caesar continues to use the formal and impersonal 'you'.

grace Reconciliation.

never/Fly off our loves again i.e. let us never be estranged again.

I must . . . ill report I must thank him otherwise I'll be accused of forgetting past favours.

Misena i.e. Misenum, a promontory in the north-west part of the Bay of Naples where in Octavius's period a harbour was created as a main base for the Roman fleet.

Would we . . . together Spoken together previously instead of arguing; I wish that we had fought Pompey before he became so strong.

to my sister's view i.e. he is invited to see Caesar's sister. Caesar is behaving with propriety and correctness.

Half the . . .Caesar cf. Plutarch who speaks of Caesar's 'two chief friends, Maecenas and Agrippa'.

digested Settled.

stayed well by 't . . . Egypt i.e. you had a good time in Egypt.

monstrous Astounding, extraordinary.

square True.

She purs'd up i.e. held captive. The metaphor is from putting money in the purse; there is also an allusion to the heart strings. Cleopatra has literally captured his heart.

river of Cydnus The river flows into the sea by the south-eastern Turkish seaboard. Tarsus, associated with St Paul, stands alongside the Cydnus. Enobarbus means that by the time Antony was by the Cydnus his heart was already 'purs'd up' by Cleopatra.

Purple the sails Note the effective inversion, and the omission of a verb.

cloth of gold, of tissue Cloth woven from gold and silk threads.

O'er-picturing Better than.

that Venus . . . nature That painting of Venus in which artistic imagination is more perfect than nature. In V,2 Cleopatra says 'Nature wants stuff/ To vie strange forms with fancy.'

Cupids Venus was the mother of the god of love, Cupid. The image links Venus and Cleopatra.

And undid did i.e. and appeared to create the warm colour on the cheeks they were cooling. Notice the repetition and reversal of 'undid did' to create the effect.

Nereides Sea-nymphs who also took human forms. They were the daughters of Nereus, the sea-god.

tended her . . . eyes Obeying her every desire; waited close to her.

bends adornings They waited on Cleopatra; their bowing, serving movements were themselves beautiful.

Swell . . . hands fun out Note again the assonontal effects dominating the lines with the emphasis upon 's' and 't' sounds, and the length of the line 'Swell with the touches of those flower-soft hands' conveying the effect of the luxurious barge with its ropes and sails swelling out.

yarely frame the office Skilfully carry out the task.

A strange . . . perfume i.e. Cleopatra's charisma, her magic.

The city . . . upon her i.e. Cleopatra's magnetism, her attraction even affects the river banks and causes the population of a city to go and look at her.

Whistling to the air i.e. doing nothing. There is an ironical contrast between Cleopatra, a magnetic centre of attraction, and Antony sitting alone – Emperor of an empty market-place.

Being barber'd ten times o'er Another reference to Antony's beard. Also the sense of being well-dressed and with hair immaculate for the occasion.

his ordinary The price of his meal.

pays his heart . . . only Marvellous contrasts between 'pays', 'heart', 'eyes' and eating, to convey Cleopatra's effect upon him.

great Caesar i.e. Julius Caesar.

she cropped Cleopatra gave birth to Caesar's son – Caesarion.

That So that.

breathless, power breathe forth i.e. her very lack of breath made her attractive. There is a pun on 'breathless' and 'breathe' – (a) they are opposites (b) 'breathe' suggests sexual attractions and charms (c) 'breathless' suggests sexual exhaustion.

Age cannot wither her i.e. Cleopatra is immortal, her beauty is eternal.

custom stale . . . variety i.e. The getting used to her will not destroy her uniqueness. Notice the contrast between 'stale' and 'variety'.

Become themselves Look becoming.

If . . . modesty i.e. the traditional ideal wifely virtues.

settle Rest, calm, satisfy.

Act II Scene 3

Antony tells Octavia in Caesar's presence that his public duties will take him away from her. She will pray for him at such times. Antony then confronts the Soothsayer, who tells him that in the exchanges with Caesar Antony's fortunes will be less than Caesar's. Dismissing the Soothsayer, Antony thinks about his words, and reverses his previous promises to Caesar. He then decides to return to Egypt where 'my pleasure lies'.

Commentary

The lack of emotion between Antony and Octavia is all too evident and they are shown together only in Caesar's presence. Octavia will do her duty. Antony's preoccupation is with politics; indeed, he even wishes his newly-married wife 'Good night', thus suggesting that there is no physical passion between them.

The Soothsayer can be regarded as a projection of Antony's subconscious fears about Caesar's good fortune. His presence deepens the atmosphere of the play and suggests ominous warnings of impending disaster. Antony's sudden change of mood and attitude, his decision to reverse his oaths, reflects both his own insecurity, the power of the Soothsayer and the hold Cleopatra has upon him. Note the contrasting imagery of demonology, 'natural luck' and almost fatalistic sensuality. He says: 'though I make this marriage for my peace,/I'the east my pleasure lies.' Antony's 'peace' is political, his peace of mind and 'pleasure' personal and beyond the Empire he normally controls. Where he is ruler, i.e. within the Roman Empire, no personal satisfaction is to be found.

The world . . . bosom Antony's order of priorities is interesting. World affairs, administration come before Octavia's physical attractions. The lines are ironic, placed after the preceding scene in which (a) Cleopatra's sensuality has been emphasized (b) Antony entered into an agreement not to neglect Octavia. They anticipate Antony's subsequent actions in which he decides to leave Octavia and Rome for Egypt and Cleopatra.

kept my square Kept straight, behaved correctly (metaphor from the carpenter's implement, a set-square).

by the rule Properly (again a metaphor from the carpenter's implements).

sirrah A contemptuous form of address used to a social inferior.

My . . . tongue I visualize it in my mind but am unable to express it. **motion** mind.

fortunes . . . higher i.e. on the wheel of fortune.

demon Guardian angel.

natural luck i.e. a gift of the gods given to some and not to others. In this case to Caesar but not to Antony.

Thy lustre thickens Your personal radiance is dulled.

art or hap Skill or luck.

faints . . . chance i.e. is defeated by his luck.

When . . . to nought When all the odds are in my favour, to my advantage.

quails Fighting birds, like pheasants.

inhoop'd, at odds Encircled, so forced to fight within the ring or cock-pit.

lies A pun: (a) to tell an untruth (b) to lie down in a resting position.

commission's i.e. your task sanctioned by my authority.

Act II Scene 4

A brief 10-line scene between soldiers leaving for battle. Agrippa says that shortly after Antony will kiss his wife he'll also be off to battle. Lepidus says he has things to do before joining up two days later with his allies at the Mount.

Commentary

A transition scene illustrating hasty war preparations and the effects upon individual lives. It serves to illustrate what action is actually being prepared against Pompey.

Trouble yourselves . . . further i.e. he dismisses them.
Mount i.e. Mount Misenum.
draw me . . . about Cause me to take a longer way.

Act II Scene 5

Back at Cleopatra's court, where she is restless, displeased and uncertain: she asks for music, then billiards, then wishes to fish in the Nile. Her mind continually dwells on Antony. The arrival of a messenger from Rome seems to confirm the worst fears that Antony is dead. She threatens the messenger with dire consequences if he brings bad news but hardly gives him a chance to tell his message. She all but faints upon hearing of the marriage between Antony and Octavia. Angrily she hits the messenger and draws a knife. Persuaded to return if, as Cleopatra hopes, his news has been mistaken, the messenger flees when her fury is once again vented on him. At the end of the scene, Alexas is sent by Cleopatra to find out from the messenger about Octavia's appearance.

Commentary

There are several things of interest in this scene. It is a contrast in tone, atmosphere and character grouping to the previous scene. Cleopatra and her immediate circle languishing in wait contrast with the brief soldierly activity. Cleopatra's changeability and moodiness are clearly demonstrated, as is the power of her imagination which is concentrated on the absent Antony. She is a powerful Empress but powerless whilst her love is away. Allusions from classical history and mythology pinpoint her dilemma. Cleopatra's reference to Philippi evokes Roman history and Antony and Octavius Caesar's defeat of a previous rebellion within the Empire, and the myth of Hercules, Antony's ancestor, who wore female clothing. A subsequent reference to Narcissus suggests self-absorption and personal hedonism. Although the fishing incident in lines 10–18 is found in Plutarch, Shakespeare transforms it into an image of Cleopatra's destructive power. She is waiting by the Nile for

Antony, whom she will 'hang', possess and catch. Her love is cruel, destructive and all-possessive.

Cleopatra's behaviour towards the messenger is moody, violent and dramatically effective. Having absolute power of life and death she plays with him. Her violent language and physical assaults upon him reflect her own emotional unbalance provoked by Antony's absence. The messenger's announcement is also delayed for reasons of dramatic suspense. The stage directions are explicit. She 'strikes him down . . . strikes him . . . hales him up and down' and then draws a knife.

moody A pun: melancholy; musical key.

trade in A further example of an image relating human affections to business activities. There is also the implication of love's being a game in which real feelings are not involved. Cleopatra's words would then be ironic for she has developed genuine feelings for Antony.

billiards In a play by Chapman, *The Blind Beggar of Alexandria* (1598), billiards is referred to as a game played by ladies in Egypt.

will Intentions; a quibble on 'well'.

come too short He, the Eunuch, doesn't play billiards well; is sexually inadequate.

The actor may plead pardon i.e. for not performing well.

none i.e. billiards.

mine angle Fishing rod; Cleopatra will search for love.

music playing far off Literally, the court music; figuratively, the source of love, Antony.

tires Head-dresses.

Then put my . . . Phillipan There are various layers of meaning here. (a) 'his sword Phillipan' refers to the sword used by Antony when he defeated Brutus and Cassius at the battle of Philippi. (See *Julius Caesar*, Act V.) In this instance Antony was the active dominant element. (b) Antony's ancestor Hercules was entrapped by Omphale. He wore her clothing, she his lion-skin and carried his weapon, a club. In this instance Antony's ancestor was not the active partner. By implication Cleopatra takes possession of Antony while he lies asleep drunk.

Ram A pun: (1) to do something quickly; (2) the male animal.

yield Report.

we use . . . well i.e. the dead are blessed since they are in heaven.

Fury In Greek mythology the Furies were the goddesses of vengeance.

formal A normally shaped man; a sane person.

good precedence The good that has gone before.

pack of matter A metaphor from a pedlar's (travelling salesman's) pack or bag, i.e. his whole stock.

whipp'd with wire Prostitutes were treated in this way.

lingering pickle A pickle made of salt or acid used to try to cure venereal disease.

boot thee i.e. give you a reward.

Thy modesty can beg i.e. any request you make will not appear to me excessive.

innocents (a) not guilty ones (b) fools.

kindly Natural creatures rather than serpents.

host of tongues Sufficient explanation.

be felt i.e. happen.

hold there still Keep to this opinion and position.

cistern Cesspool. Notice the alliteration emphasizing the fierceness: 'cistern', 'scald', 'snakes'.

Hadst thou . . . most ugly i.e. even if you were as beautiful as Narcissus I would still regard you as ugly.

Narcissus A youth in Grecian mythology famous for his good looks. He fell in love with his own reflection in a pool and pined away and died because his love was doomed to be unfulfilled.

O that his . . . sure of I wish that Antony's trickery could also make you as dishonest as he.

Lie they upon thy hand Let them remain unsold.

feature Appearance.

painted one way . . . i.e. things may be viewed from different angles.

Gorgon There were three Gorgons – the snake-haired monsters of Greek mythology. One was Medusa, slain by Perseus. It was said that the sight of her head turned viewers to stone.

Act II Scene 6

The two warring factions meet at Mount Misenum and exchange hostages. They agree on peace terms and depart to make arrangements to 'feast each other ere we part'. Menas and Enobarbus remain on stage, and the banter between them concerning mutual thievery gives way to serious commentary. Menas is perplexed by Antony's marriage to Caesar's sister which will 'knit' them 'together'. Menas regards Antony as unreliable and regrets that Pompey has made peace with the triumvirate. Enobarbus too believes that Antony will return to his old Egyptian love Cleopatra.

Commentary

The stage is initially crowded with male soldiers, providing an effective contrast in tone and setting with the previous Egyptian feminine, but far from passive, female-dominated stage presence. Previous references to meeting at Mount Misenum are realized and preparations made for the subsequent dramatic scenes aboard Pompey's galley. The first 83 lines of poetry are concerned with reconciliation between enemies. The subject is politics and past events which split the Roman Empire asunder. Notice that Cleopatra cannot be kept out of affairs. Antony confesses to Pompey that 'The beds i' the east are soft', and she is the focus of Enobarbus's remarks relating to Caesar's seduction of her in line 70. She becomes the central focus of the prose commentary between the two 'minor' characters Enobarbus and Menas, who are left on stage after the others have departed. Enobarbus's insights into Antony's character and his awareness of Cleopatra's power over him are further revealed. Menas also displays much insight. Enobarbus's imagery of coldness, heat and food to describe the complex inter-relationships between Octavia and Antony, Octavia and Caesar, Antony and Cleopatra, are other examples of images present throughout the play.

tall Brave.

To you . . . world i.e. the three triumvirs.

factors Agents.

ghosted i.e. visited as a ghost. Julius Caesar's ghost appeared to Brutus before the battle of Philippi. Pompey is saying that the assassination of Julius Caesar was avenged at Philippi so why shouldn't Pompey avenge his father? (His father, Pompey the Great, escaped to Egypt after being defeated by Julius Caesar and was put to death in Egypt.)

Cassius The chief conspirator against Julius Caesar.

courtiers Lovers.

drench i.e. with blood (not rain).

Capitol In Shakespeare's *Julius Caesar*, Caesar was killed in the Capitol (the Roman Parliament).

one man but a man? i.e. no dictators: one man should not be that more powerful than others.

is it i.e. the reason why.

sails i.e. ships, an example of *synecdoche* (Greek for 'taking together'), where the part of something is used to signify the whole (e.g. 'ten hands' for ten workers).

speak with A euphemism for 'fight with'.

o'er-count Outnumber; deprive, do me out of. This word is used twice, first by Antony then by Pompey, thus constituting a delayed pun.

But since the . . . mayst But since like the cuckoo you have stolen another person's nest, remain in it as long as you can. Pompey is threatening Antony; perhaps also insinuating that Antony is being cuckolded by Cleopatra.

For this is . . . present i.e. this is irrelevant to the present business and concerns.

And what . . . larger fortune i.e. and what the consequences may be if you start a war.

edges i.e. of our swords (weapons).

targes Shields.

your brother i.e. Lucius Antonius. Pompey is now talking to Antony.

mother i.e. Julia, Julius Caesar's sister who fled with Fulvia and was helped by Pompey.

counts Reckonings.

casts upon Flings against.

crave our composition Request that our agreement.

take the lot i.e. accept the decision of the lottery.

fine Egyptian cookery Suggestive words relating by implication to Antony's relationship with Cleopatra.

grew fat with feasting there Note the alliterative 'f' and 't' sounds reinforcing the reminder (a painful one for Antony) of Julius Caesar's past relationship with Cleopatra.

And fair words to them i.e. make sure you speak your thoughts.

Apollodorous A further use of Plutarch, who relates how Apollodorous, Cleopatra's servant, disguised her by rolling her in a mattress. She was then carried to Caesar in Alexandria.

A certain queen Notice that Enobarbus in an effort to tone down the situation, which must be provoking Antony, doesn't use Cleopatra's name.

I know thee now Pompey pretends that he has just recognized Enobarbus.

like Likely.

I deny my land service A quibble: (a) I claim to be exempt from serving in the army; (b) I deny that I have been a land thief.

authority Power to arrest (as constables) – an interesting metaphor for the 'eyes'.

take i.e. arrest.

kissing i.e. (a) making friends (b) clasping hands.

fair woman A pun: honest, decent; attractive physically; a reference to Cleopatra and by contrast Octavia. Notice that a few lines previously Pompey and Antony quibbled with 'fair meanings' and 'fair words'.

a true face i.e. a face without make-up; the face reveals the thoughts.

he cannot weep't back again i.e. when he realizes too late the error he has made. Note that in the next scene Menas suggests to Pompey that he use the party as an opportunity to get rid of his rivals.

Pray he sir? Is this really so?

the policy . . . parties Political reasons for the marriage greater than the love between Antony and Octavia.

band Bond of unity.

still Subdued.

conversation Way of life.

that which i.e. Octavia.

for you i.e. to drink to.

us'd our throats i.e. got used to drinking.

Act II Scene 7

On board Pompey's galley near Misenum. Two servants comment on the activities of Caesar, Antony, Pompey and Lepidus,
together for a reconciliation banquet. Whilst the others drink and
enjoy themselves Menas attempts to draw Pompey aside. At last
he manages to suggest that Antony, Caesar and Lepidus are in
Pompey's power and should be slaughtered. The idea appeals to
Pompey, but he rejects it on the grounds that his honour will be
stained if the plan goes ahead; however, if he hadn't known about
it his approval would have been forthcoming. Menas is stung by
the reply and vows no longer to serve Pompey. Lepidus is
removed in a drunken, insensible state. The revels continue with
dancing, music and a Bacchanalian song. The relatively sober
Caesar takes his leave. Pompey reminds Antony of a dispute
between them (relating to Antony's occupation of Pompey's
father's house) and adds 'but what, we are friends', and the party
breaks up.

Commentary

Points to note in this central scene are: its stage presentation and
construction; the way in which the drunken orgy provides an
allegory for the disintegration of the Roman world, as well as
underlining the chief protagonists' natures; the way in which
every word, gesture and action is made to seem significant.

The prologue, between the first and second servant, sets the
scene and allows for the stage furniture to be arranged, and in
addition provides a commentary on the succeeding action. There
is a threefold division in the scene. The first servant's opening
comment 'Some o' their plants are ill-rooted already, the least
wind i' the world will blow them down' alludes to the hypocrisy of
the alliance between warring factions that has just taken place,
and to the actual drunkenness to follow where 'the least wind'
literally blows down triumvirs. Again the first servant's 'To be
called into a huge sphere, and not to be seen to move in't, are the
holes where eyes should be, which pitifully disaster the cheeks',
points to a lack of vision and insight, to cosmic disintegration, and
to hollowness. If the rulers of the Roman Empire cannot keep
steady legs and control themselves, then how can the subjects of
that Empire control themselves?

The threefold construction provides a commentary on meaning and action. In the first part the reconciled triumvirs engage in
hollow frivolities, getting more and more drunk. In the second

part Menas reveals his treacherous plan to destroy the others. In the third, begun by the removal of the insensible drunken Lepidus, a chaotic uncontrolled orgy occurs. The parts are linked by Menas's attempt at conspiracy. In the first he attempts in vain to gain Pompey's attention while the main dialogue, Antony's mock lecture on the crocodile told by the drunk Lepidus, proceeds. So there is on stage, a scene within a scene. Audience attention is drawn away from the main revellers to focus upon two of them. Antony's remark (line 58) to Lepidus concerning 'These quick-sands . . ./Keep off them, for you sink' have a special significance. Lepidus literally does 'sink' into drunkenness (line 87).

Antony's 'quicksands' refers to the kind of conspiracy Menas is suggesting to Pompey. Double standards are at work. Pompey would have welcomed Menas's murder plot provided he hadn't heard about it. Roman concepts of honour and dignity are exposed as a shallow pretence. Menas wants the world 'to go on wheels' – the physical sensations in his head reflecting an actual state of affairs in the Empire. Lepidus, triumvir who 'bears the third part of the world' is borne away from the party insensible: 'The third part then is drunk.'

plants A pun: (1) seeds; (2) soles of the feet.

wind i' the world Any kind of breeze; any disturbance within the Roman Empire.

alms-drink A reference to the custom of a drunkard's place in toasting being taken by another in order to answer the toast; the liquor dregs saved for the very poor – the alms drinkers (by implication Lepidus has lost control of himself and will be stripped of all he possesses).

pinch one . . . disposition i.e. the more they drink the more troublesome they become arguing with one another.

'No more' Note the irony. The servant notes that Lepidus has spoken out in an effort perhaps to stop the personal quarrelling. On the other hand they are (perhaps with the exception of Lepidus, who is too drunk to drink) still drinking!

But it raises . . . discretion Although Lepidus makes peace between the arguing other drinkers the effort involved creates a conflict between his desires and what his body can take (in the way of drink).

a reed . . . service A startling image of insignificance.

partisan I . . . heave i.e. a useless long-handled two-headed spear I'm unable to throw.

To be called into a . . . cheeks The speech uses an astronomical metaphor. The servant says that to be placed in a position of high authority and not to exercise its functions and duties, like a star which fails to orbit, is comparable to a face with empty eye-sockets. Notice the correspondence between (a) the human body (b) the state of the Roman

Empire (c) the cosmos, the universe. In effect this short prose speech provides a commentary on the actions of the play.

disaster Ruin, disfigure. Disaster is a word of astrological origin, reminiscent of the expression 'the stars are against me'.

cheeks The human face; life itself (metaphorically).

sennet Trumpet notes announcing the arrival (or departure) of important people.

take the flow Measure the rising.

scales i' the pyramid Markings on the pyramid. The pyramid refers to a special pillar used for measurements, as well as to the well-known pyramids.

foison Plenty. This opens a series of images of fertility.

comes to i.e. it comes – the grain.

your serpent . . . sun A reference to the belief in spontaneous generation, in this instance that serpents were created from the mud; an implied suggestion that Cleopatra is now sleeping with low life creatures; the sun that shines on Antony shines on the mud and also on Cleopatra.

crocodile Crocodiles enjoy the slime and the mud. They are destructive creatures. Lepidus is calling Cleopatra a crocodile.

I'll ne'er out i.e. I'll not back away from making a toast.

I fear me . . . then i.e. until you have slept.

Ptolomies' pyramises (a) a reference back to the servant's speech about the 'huge sphere' and its reference to the Ptolomaic astronomical system: Lepidus couldn't have heard this speech; (b) pyramises – Lepidus's intoxicated plural of 'pyramis' (the singular form) – conveys drunken speech patterns. Notice the assonant 'p' and 's' sounds with their repetitive effect.

elements i.e. of life, or earth, air, fire and water. Antony is being humorous. The comedy depends upon the implications of 'It' and the 'Crocodile'.

transmigrates i.e. its soul passes into something else's body.

tears of . . . are wet The crocodile was supposed to cry over its victims.

I have ever . . . fortunes I have served you loyally.

Wilt thou . . . world? Dramatically most effective, for one of the triumvirs is literally sinking to the ground.

pales Encloses.

put off i.e. at sea.

All there is thine Menas probably gestures towards the drunken triumvirs. He could also be referring expansively to the world. The words and gesture are not without irony; is that *all* Pompey will inherit – a drunken unruly crowd!?

Mine honour, it My honour is more important than my personal pursuit of power.

unknown i.e. to me.

pall'd Enfeebled.

cup be hid i.e. until it is so full you can no longer see the inside of the cup.

bears . . . world Ironic – Lepidus, the triumvir, is insensible through drink. Yet he has responsibility for a third of the world!

go on wheels Go more speedily and smoothly.

the reels Revels – enjoyment; a play on 'wheels' and 'reels'.

Alexandrian feast i.e. like those at the court of Cleopatra. Cf. II, 2 where, according to Enobarbus 'we did sleep day out of countenance, and make the night light with drinking'.

Strike the vessels Empty the casks; fill the cups to the full. Notice that Antony seems to have forgotten that he is not the host.

monstrous Unnatural.

wash my . . . fouler i.e. with wine and odours. The force of 'it' draws attention to Caesar's distaste for what is happening.

Be a . . . time i.e. do what everyone else is doing.

Possess it, I'll make answer Possess the time rather than be mastered by it, and pledge the toast.

Egyptian Bacchanals Riotous drunken dances and orgies celebrating the Roman god of wine Bacchus.

Lethe The river of Hades. Drinking its waters brought oblivion.

The holding . . . bear (Every man shall) sing the chorus.

pink eyne Eyes red from drinking.

fats Vats (of wine).

Good brother i.e. Antony.

Splits . . . speaks Mispronounces, doesn't speak properly.

disguise i.e. the drunken dance and associated activities.

Antick'd Made a fool of.

I'll try . . . the shore i.e. I'll test how much drink you can take when on shore.

You have my father's house Pompey is unable to forget his grievances against Antony.

Neptune The Roman god of the sea.

There's my cap (He) throws it in the air.

Revision questions on Act II

1 What does Act II tell us about Cleopatra's personality?

2 Write a detailed analysis of Enobarbus's description of Cleopatra in Scene 2 (lines 190–218).

3 What is the nature of the conflict between (a) Caesar and Antony (b) Pompey and Antony?

4 Describe and comment upon the dramatic construction of Scene 7.

5 Discuss the view that 'contrasts and comparisons reverberate throughout the second Act'.

Act III Scene 1

On the Syrian plain the Romans led by Ventidius (dispatched to Parthia at the end of II, 3) have defeated the Parthians. Ventidius has killed Pacorus, the son of the Parthian King, and thus revenged the treacherous slaying of the triumvir Marcus Crassus. Ventidius resists Silius's promptings to pursue the fleeing Parthians. Ventidius is tired of fighting and doesn't wish to steal too much of the limelight and hence place his General and Commander Antony in the shade.

Commentary

This scene on the battlefield away from Rome and Egypt on the outer fringes of the Empire brilliantly contrasts with the previous scene. Ventidius and Silius cannot indulge in drunken orgies, they have to defeat the enemies of the disintegrating corrupt triumvirate. Ventidius's actions reveal the power of Rome. On the other hand the waning of Antony's power is revealed. He is known as 'the word of war'; the realities are that others do Antony's fighting for him and Antony merely takes the credit. Ventidius's modesty and reluctance to pursue his victory show true wisdom, for he knows that those at the top such as Antony cannot stomach competition.

darting Parthia i.e. casting or firing arrows. The Parthians were famous for shooting arrows from horseback especially when riding away from a charge.

struck Echoes 'darting'.

Marcus Crassus' death A triumvirate with Julius Caesar and the elder Pompey of the previous generation. Parleying with Surenas, general of King Orodes of Parthia's army, after being defeated, he was murdered. Crassus's mouth was filled with molten gold by Orodes who was mocking Crassus's obsession with gold. Orodes was the father of the dead Pacorus whose body is borne before Ventidius.

Media Today north-western Iran, south of the Caspian Sea.

Mesopotamia Literally 'between the rivers' – Tigris and Euphrates – at the northern tip of the Persian Gulf in modern day Iraq. The distance of Media and Mesopotamia from Rome reveals just how extensively spread Roman influence was in the ancient world.

garlands The Roman symbol of victory in battle.

O Silius . . . enough Note the elegiac, philosophical, battle-weary tone conveyed in the repetition of 'Silius' and the simplicity of the language.

A lower place . . . great an act i.e. a person in a subordinate position should not be so successful that his superior will feel threatened.

in their officer Through their subordinate officers.

Sossius A Roman commander who, with Herod, took Jerusalem and led Antigonus as a prisoner to Antony.

my place i.e. of the same rank, a subordinate.

rather makes ... darkens him i.e. decides it's better to accept a loss, than a gain the consequences of which will lead to disfavour, for the commander will thus be placed in the shade.

his offence By offending him (Antony).

my performance perish My achievements be wasted.

That magical word of war i.e. Antony's name inspiring soldiers.

his banners ... his well-paid The repetition of 'his' reinforces where the limelight is – on Antony.

weight Several meanings here, e.g. the army and its supplies; the booty; captives plus the dead Pacorus.

Act III Scene 2

At Caesar's house Agrippa and Enobarbus mock the unity of the triumvirate and express very little faith in Caesar and Antony. Enobarbus's impression of Lepidus is very low. The triumvirate return to the stage with Caesar and Antony expressing mutual trust. Caesar is troubled in parting from his sister and asks Antony to treat her well. Brother and sister talk together, and what she says brings tears to Caesar's eyes. Enobarbus notes that tears are not appropriate to soldiers. Agrippa reminds him that Antony too has cried. Caesar and Octavia bid farewell.

Commentary

There are five areas of interest in this scene. First of all there is an expression of genuine love between brother and sister which conflicts with the claims of political expediency. Secondly, Caesar in his parting from Octavia realizes that political factors are more important than personal feelings and considerations. Thirdly, Antony's rhetoric with his use of the interesting 'the swan's down feather' image and the sea is somewhat ironic. The irony lies not merely in his subsequent actions – he returns to Cleopatra and deserts Octavia – but also in his past actions when he suppressed personal emotions in *Julius Caesar* and praised Julius Caesar's murderers. Fourthly, the cynicism of the subordinates Agrippa and Enobarbus further exposes the follies of the rulers of the Roman Empire: Enobarbus's description of Lepidus as a beetle is particularly effective. Fifthly, the scene's imagery, character pairings and situations present a balance of forces, thereby providing a commentary on the action. Brother and sister are balanced against husband and wife; Agrippa and Enobarbus balance each other. The weak, insignificant triumvir speaks but two lines at the end of the scene. Octavia's metaphorical feather balances in the tide, Antony and Caesar are locked in a power struggle represented by the wrestling image.

sad Serious.

is troubled with, . . . sickness A witty reference to a form of anaemia supposed to affect young girls in love. Its characteristics were supposed to be tiredness and the wish to eat chalk and lime!

Jupiter See note p.38.

nonpareil Without equal.

Arabian bird A reference to the Phoenix, the mythical Arabian bird, only one of which was ever alive at one time. It was supposed to live for five to six hundred years, burn itself, and to rise from its own ashes to begin again a cycle of fresh life.

But he loves . . . Antony The line nicely balances Caesar and Antony and reflects the power struggle taking place between the two.

figures i.e. of speech.

cast See note 'casts upon', p.47.

number Write verses.

hearts, tongues . . . number Notice that each of the nouns – 'hearts, tongues, . . .' corresponds to a verb in the following line. Such a device was not uncommon in Elizabethan poetry. Perhaps Shakespeare, through Enobarbus, is parodying the device.

Kneel down . . . down The repetition serves to emphasize Caesar's power.

shards The beetle's horny wing-cases. In this instance the beetle's wings are meant.

their beetle i.e. Lepidus is Antony's and Caesar's beetle.

a great part of myself i.e. Octavia.

my thoughts make thee As I (Caesar) expect you to be.

as my farthest . . . approof My utmost bond shall pledge to be (i.e. such a wife as I think you will be).

piece of virtue Octavia.

ram Battering-ram.

mean Means; go-between.

therein curious Careful.

The April's in her . . . it on According to Roman mythology April with its showers was special to Venus: her wet radiant eyes were symbols of love. Antony is indulging in rhetorical fancy.

Her tongue . . . tongue i.e. she is unable to find words to express what she really wishes to say.

the swan's down feather . . . way inclines A powerful and suggestive image. Antony compares Octavia's emotions with a feather entrapped by cross-currents as the tide is just about to turn. By implication Antony and Caesar are the cross-currents, and Octavia is the feather. She is pulled between her husband and her brother; her real emotions and her duty; speech and silence.

He were the . . . a horse A horse which didn't have a white mark on its face was regarded as sullied or blemished.

When Antony . . . slain Allusions to past Roman events, which are described in *Julius Caesar*.

rheum A head cold, which caused his eyes to run.

Let all . . . fair way Remember that in this scene Lepidus has until now remained silent.

Act III Scene 3

This scene is a continuation of Act II Scene 5. Cleopatra's messenger returns but is afraid of her. His report on Octavia is unfavourable. She is shorter than Cleopatra, has a lower voice, walks more like a statue than a live person. Octavia is old enough to be a widow and has a round face and brown hair, with a low forehead. Cleopatra has a message to give to her messenger.

Commentary

Cleopatra and her reactions are the focal points of attention. Genuine human emotions rather than political expediency and false emotions are once again in the limelight. The scene doesn't, however, lack irony. Appearance and viewpoint play an important part in it. Cleopatra is obsessed with her rival's appearance and reveals a range of reactions to what she is told. At first she is out of humour, then jealous, then disparaging, then satisfied. The messenger's comment that Octavia is not as tall as she Cleopatra translates into 'dwarfish'. Her messenger tells his mistress what will please her.

Herod of Jewry See note p.25. This suggests that Cleopatra enters in a virulent mood.

Herod's head Antony has beheaded Antigonus, the last of the Jewish Kings actively to resist Roman rule.

I looked . . . face Suggesting that the messenger is afraid to look into Cleopatra's face and is cowering away from her.

Remember/If e'er . . . majesty i.e. as you have seen me you know what Majesty is. Cleopatra has a very high opinion of herself.

station i.e. her position with Antony.

Three in Egypt i.e. Cleopatra, Charmian, Iras. Note the ironic contrast if they are compared with the Roman triumvirate.

she's thirty Cleopatra is thirty-eight!

Round . . . faultiness Cleopatra believes that round faces denote foolishness.

her forehead . . . it High foreheads were considered signs of great beauty, low ones of ordinariness.

Our The royal plural.

harried Ill-treated.

This creature's . . . thing Octavia's nothing very much.

Isis else defend Isis stop it from being otherwise.

Act III Scene 4

Antony is at Athens, the headquarters of his eastern command. Antony complains that Caesar has attacked Pompey and spoken disrespectfully of himself. Octavia begs her husband to think well of her brother, otherwise she will be torn between the two. Antony tells her to choose the one she feels will best look after her, and takes a rather cool farewell of her.

Commentary

Shakespeare treats his source Plutarch, the basis for this scene, selectively. Antony in Athens is one step nearer to Egypt and Cleopatra. The reality of Antony's relationship with Octavia is shown and provides a contrast with Cleopatra's speculations in the previous scene. Octavia's dilemma and isolation are seen in her monologue, where she is overheard by the audience expressing to herself her problems. She is torn between husband and brother. Her role as a reconciling factor has proved useless. Her internal problems are reflected on a wider scale: the two powerful triumvirs are at loggerheads and the Roman Empire is split apart. It is impossible for Octavia to steer a middle course. She has to make a choice. Personal commitment is one of the themes of the play.

semblable Similar.

made . . . public ear i.e. in the manner of Julius Caesar, who made a will in the people's favour and hence gained general support.

When the best hint . . . teeth i.e. when the opportunity presented itself to praise me he gave token rather than whole-hearted praise.

stomach Resent.

A more unhappy lady . . . at all Not spoken to Antony, who has engaged his attentions elsewhere, but overheard by the audience.

If this division chance If the relationship should break up.

branchless i.e. with my honour taken from me – cut away as branches from a tree.

stain Place in the shade.
As if the . . . the rift Note the startling vision of the Roman Empire split asunder by civil war and united only by killings: the slain men soldering up 'the rift'.
where this begins i.e. who starts the conflict.

Act III Scene 5

Enobarbus and Eros, a slave of Antony, discuss events. Caesar and Lepidus have made war on Pompey; after the victory Lepidus has been discarded, arrested and held in prison. Pompey has been murdered by one of Antony's men – an action which has incensed Antony. Enobarbus is wanted by Antony.

Commentary

This scene conveys information, summarizes political events and repeats some of what the audience already know. Caesar's manipulative ruthlessness is illustrated through his treatment of Lepidus. Antony's insecurity and uncertainties show themselves in his regret for actions taken by his soldiers. Enobarbus's image of the Roman Empire being squabbled over by two animals feuding for a scrap of meat brilliantly sums up what is taking place. Servants and subordinates once again emerge in the play as commentators upon the actions and activities of the rulers.

the success The result.
rivality Partnership.
his own appeal i.e. his own accusation with supporting evidence.
enlarge his confine A nice antithesis, 'enlarge' and 'confine'; i.e. until death release him.
chaps Jaws.
And throw . . . other Caesar and Antony become two wild animals fighting over scraps of food.
He's walking . . . Pompey Perhaps expressed in anger by Eros against Antony's behaviour.
murdered Pompey The defeated Pompey fled east to the island of Samos where Antony's lieutenant Titius murdered him.
Domitius Enobarbus.
'Twill be naught (a) the expedition will fail, or (b) although Antony wants to see him urgently, the meeting will prove to be unimportant. Enobarbus's 'naught' is echoed at the opening of IV,10.

Act III Scene 6

The scene returns to the centre of Roman imperial power, Caesar's house. Caesar catalogues for Agrippa and Maecenas a detailed list of complaints concerning Antony's behaviour in Egypt with Cleopatra. Antony has divided his portion of the Roman Empire between his own sons. Caesar will allow him some of Lepidus's areas, but demands in return a say in the way the lands gained from Pompey are portioned out. Maecenas has his doubts as to whether Antony will agree to this.

Octavia appears without formal introduction, which provokes Caesar. She is surprised that Antony has returned to Egypt and that he is preparing to fight Caesar, having enlisted the support of many monarchs. Caesar offers his sister what comfort he can, but she is torn by the news, which she finds hard to believe.

Commentary

Alexandria and Athens have given way to Rome, although part of the scene recounts Antony's and Cleopatra's Egyptian activities. Caesar's political and deeply personal animosity to Antony comes clearly to the fore and is exacerbated by Octavia's appearance. The scene conveys information about Antony's personal and political activities. It reveals the extent of the Roman Empire which is being fought over. Caesar's view of Antony and Cleopatra is a biased one, and should be contrasted with that of Enobarbus. Caesar's reaction to his sister's appearance without the regal forms appropriate to her, and his shift to a personal concern, is yet another example of the transition in the play between the political and the personal. The scene is not without some scathing passages. The word 'lust' in Caesar's opening speech takes on a special force placed at the end of a line. Octavia's insignificance and her role as a political pawn are neatly summed up by Caesar's 'Being an abstract 'tween his lust and him'. Caesar's comment that Antony 'hath given his empire/ Up to a whore' may be regarded by many as all too true.

tribunal silver'd A silver-plated dais. The phrase is in North's Plutarch.
Caesarion i.e. Julius Caesar's son by Cleopatra (see II, 2, 228).
father's son Julius Caesar adopted Octavius.
stablishment Government.
Lower Syria Modern day Israel, northern Lebanon and Syria.
Cyprus The Mediterranean island.
Lydia Plutarch wrote 'Lybia' (on the North African Mediterranean

coast); however North wrote 'Lydia' (the middle portion of the Asia Minor western coast). Shakespeare copied North.

Absolute queen Notice that Caesar indicates that Antony is giving to Cleopatra and her heirs portions of the Roman Empire.

Armenia Now in the USSR, between Asia Minor and the Caspian Sea.

Cilicia An area in south-east Asia Minor. The river Cydnus was in Cilicia.

  Phoenicia South of Beirut, the coastline of Lebanon.

habiliments Robes.

spoil'd Overthrown.

  rated Granted.

revenue Lepidus's possessions.

change i.e. replacement, imprisonment.

castaway Ruined woman.

expectation Those waiting.

A market-maid i.e. in a humble, unshowy manner. Notice that Caesar is still thinking of the diplomatic usage he can make of his sister.

which, left unshown . . . left unlov'd A profound remark: love unshown and unspoken can die.

pardon Permission.

an abstract . . . and him Octavia has been the symbol of what is stopping Antony from indulging his lust.

have eyes upon him I am (probably through spies) watching him.

nodded Called him. The word suggests that Antony is Cleopatra's slave, obeying her every 'nod'.

He hath . . . whore . . . for war A magnificent expression conveying Caesar's utter contempt.

Libya In this instance the correct form: cf. previous note.

Cappadocia North and north-east of Cilicia in Asia Minor.

Paphlagonia On the northern side of Asia Minor or present-day Turkey, near the Russian border, on the south coast of the Black Sea.

  Thracian Thrace was an important part of the Roman Empire. Now in Bulgaria, Turkey and Greece.

King Mauchus . . . Pont Pont was a remote province of the Roman Empire in the most north-easterly part of Asia Minor. These names are taken from North's Plutarch. There has been some confusion: Polemon was king of Pont.

Comagene On the north-eastern Syrian border with the River Euphrates as the boundary.

Mede i.e. Media (today north-west Iran between the Black Sea, the Caspian Sea, and south of the Caucasus).

  Lycaonia A Roman province in southern Asia Minor. These names have little intrinsic interest. They do however represent how far flung is the disintegrating Roman Empire, how powerful Antony is in the areas he appears to control, and how wide ranging is Caesar's intelligence system (his 'eyes').

Welcome . . . welcome to us In this speech Caesar, who initially has been concerned with the political implications of Octavia's return, now shows his private feelings.

breaking forth Into hostility.

large Uncontrolled, licentious.

regiment Authority.

trull Prostitute.

Act III Scene 7

Antony's camp near Actium, where dissension emerges amongst his followers. Enobarbus tries to discourage Cleopatra from personally entering into the fight with Antony. Her presence will distract and unsettle him. Cleopatra ignores his advice, as does Antony when Enobarbus disagrees with his intentions to engage in a naval battle with Caesar. A soldier also urges Antony not to fight Caesar by sea. Antony will not listen and is determined to keep to his plan of attack, especially as Cleopatra has offered naval assistance. Antony is amazed by the news of Caesar's rapid advances.

Commentary

Cleopatra's and Antony's stubbornness clearly emerge in this scene. She ignores Enobarbus, an experienced adviser. The battlefield, he says, is not the place for personal passion but for masculine combat. Notice the self-destructive impulses in Antony; he ignores the words of his closest advisers. An experienced soldier tells his 'noble emperor ... Trust not to rotten planks' – a very brave comment given the hierarchical Roman system where everyone had his place. Of course the soldier turns out to be correct, so his assonant words (the 't' repetition should not go unnoticed) act as an anticipatory device prefiguring what is to happen in the drama.

forspoke Spoken against.

if not denounc'd against us War was declared against Cleopatra as Head of State and not against Antony.

serve A pun: serve in the army; copulate.

horse i.e. stallions.

merely Utterly.

What is 't you say? Cleopatra hasn't heard (or perhaps incredulously has) Enobarbus's crudities.

Take from ... time i.e. make demands upon his emotions, his mind and his time.

Traduc'd Blamed.

levity Not paying attention to his responsibilities.

Photinus Photinus in fact brought about the murder of Pompey the Great.

Sink Rome A marvellously dismissive pair of words: assumedly she wants the city to subside into the Tiber. The words echo Antony's 'Let Rome in Tiber melt' (I, 1).

Tartentum, and Brundusium The modern Taranto and Brindisi, one on each side of the Italian 'heel'.

Ionian Sea Off Actium (the site of the impending battle), the sea off the Greek west coast.

Toryne In Macedonia.

admir'd Wondered at.

Pharsalia About 80 km (50 m) to the south of Mount Olympus in Greece.

Ingross'd Conscripted by the press gang.

yare Light, quick on their feet.

head of Actium The northernmost tip of the north-western Greek coast.

descried Caught sight of.

Thetis In mythology a sea-nymph, and goddess mother of Achilles. This is a compliment to Cleopatra who has offered ships and positive military assistance.

Do you . . . wounds? i.e. have you lost faith in your veterans?

go a-ducking (a) fall into the sea (b) behave as ducks (c) act foolishly.

Not in the . . . on 't Not from his own will-power or initiative.

Carries The metaphor is from archery, an arrow 'carries' to its resting place.

some i.e. information.

Act III Scene 8

Marching with some of his army towards the battle of Actium, Caesar commands his forces not to fight on land until the naval battle has been decided.

Commentary

The start of a sequence of brief scenes focusing upon crucial stages in the decisive battle. Caesar is decisively in command, with no opposition or questioning of his decisions. He has a carefully planned strategy.

prescript Written instructions.
jump Risk.

Act III Scene 9

Antony instructs Enobarbus to take the forces to a hillside position from which they can assess Caesar's naval strength and plan accordingly.

Commentary

Shakespeare is unable to present land conflicts or naval battles on stage; all he can do is to select crucial events. Antony's relative uncertainty contrasts with Caesar's relative confidence in the previous scene.

Act III Scene 10

Elements of the opposing armies cross and re-cross the stage. The noise of a sea battle is heard off stage. Enobarbus tells of Antony's naval defeat; of the flight of the Antoniad, Cleopatra's flagship, with sixty ships. A fellow general Scarus enters to add that Antony too has deserted the battle to follow Cleopatra. Another general Canidius also has seen Antony's actions and decides to turn his troops over to the opposition. Enobarbus, despite his good sense, will remain with Antony.

Commentary

Crucial events are reported rather than enacted. The focus is on the reaction to the events rather than the actual events themselves. Antony is not shown flying 'like a doting mallard' after Cleopatra. The 'shame' is expressed by Scarus in startling metaphors taken from nature. His scorn for Cleopatra 'Yon ribaud-red nag of Egypt' – is conveyed through images of disease, whores and ageing horses. The scene contains remarkable lines which in many ways sum up much of the play. Scarus's 'The greater cantle of the world is lost/With very ignorance, we have kiss'd away/Kingdoms, and provinces' deserves memorizing. Enobarbus's fidelity to his master Antony – against his better judgement – emerges at the end of the scene.

Naught Ruined, total loss.
admiral Flagship (in which Cleopatra sails).
synod Assembly (of gods and goddesses).
passion Distress.
token'd pestilence Skin spots which were the beginnings of the

plague, and known as God's tokens because they resembled certain tradesmen's tokens.

ribaudred nag Whorish jaded woman. A nag is an old overworked horse.

leprosy A disease associated, at that time, with whores and reputed to be common in Egypt.

When vantage . . . same When the fortunes of battle seemed balanced equally.

ours the elder Slightly to our advantage.

breeze Gadfly; wind; light and trifling – without substance.

cow Perhaps an allusion to the cow sacred to Isis. Cleopatra had been called Isis.

loof'd Turning towards the wind before preparing to change direction at sea.

Claps on his sea-wing i.e. raises his sails.

sinks most lamentably (a) the loss of the navy; (b) the wheel of the goddess Fortune. She was represented as being tossed on the waves of a stormy sea.

Been what . . . himself i.e. been true to himself.

Peloponnesus A peninsula forming the southern part of Greece, and in the direction of Egypt, where Antony and Cleopatra fled.

render Surrender.

Act III Scene 11

Back in Egypt at Cleopatra's palace Antony broods over his dishonour. He offers his followers gold as payment and incentive to desert him but they are unwilling to leave him. Cleopatra enters. Antony remembers his past glories at Philippi, where he defeated Cassius and Brutus, and compares this time with his present condition. Cleopatra collapses and tries to excuse herself. Antony recognizes that she has had total power over him. Now he has to humble himself to Caesar. However, for one of her tears the world has been well lost. He has sent their children's tutor to seek peace terms from Caesar.

Commentary

A scene of conflicting emotions, of bitter regrets and recriminations. The scene has much pathos. Antony, a man of great power, has been shamed and tamed by another. Antony is deranged and obsessed by Cleopatra. Bereft of dignity and reputation, Antony is now totally under Cleopatra's control. Memories of happier times give way to memories of misguided defeat and the desire for the affirmation of their love: 'give me a kiss,/Even this repays me' – Antony tells Cleopatra. There are superb brief comments scattered through the scene ranging from 'I/Have lost my way for ever', 'I have offended reputation/A most unnoble swerving', to 'Fall not a tear, I say, one of them rates/All that is won and lost.'

lated Belated. The metaphor is from that of a traveller overtaken by dusk.

show their shoulders i.e. turn their backs on the enemy.

that What (i.e. Cleopatra).

for the white . . . doting An interesting image from physical features. He is torn with inner conflict, even his hair which has white hairs (the signs of age and worry) reprove the brown hairs (signs of youth and virility). A paradox between brown and white, age and youth.

hint Opportunity.

Let that be . . . itself i.e. leave the man whose senses have left him.

possess you Give to you.

Leave me . . . I pray you Notice that Antony's self-absorption partly conveyed through the repetition of the pronoun 'I' suggests also that his attendants are unwilling to leave him by himself.

Juno Roman goddess, wife of Jupiter.

Yes my lord Antony is fantasizing, speaking to an imaginary lord.

he Caesar.

Philippi The battle at which Caesar and Antony defeated Brutus and Cassius.

sword e'en like a dancer i.e. for decorative purposes and not for use.

lean . . . Cassius cf. *Julius Caesar*, I, 2, 'Yon Cassius hath a lean and hungry look.'

mad Brutus ended A curious remark. Brutus was noted for his integrity, idealism and belief in principles.

Dealt on lieutenantry Let his lieutenants do his fighting for him.
  practice Experience.

squares i.e. battle formation (the Romans preferred to fight in square troop formations).

is unqualitied Has lost his self-respect.

Egypt Notice that Antony doesn't address her as 'Cleopatra' but in the form of addressing a country, 'Egypt'.
  See . . . eyes . . . looking back See how I remove myself and my dishonour from your sight by being alone and reflecting upon the past.

You Cleopatra addresses him in the deferential 'You' form, implying apology, and assuring him that he is in the superior position.

palter Shuffle, play tricks.

a tear . . . lost An effective antithesis between one single tear and the control of the Roman Empire.

our schoolmaster i.e. their children's tutor.

full of lead Heavy with grief.

we scorn her . . . blows We scorn fortune when she is at her most
forceful and terrible.

Act III Scene 12

Caesar and his forces are already in Egypt. The schoolmaster
arrives in Caesar's camp to act as Antony's messenger. His
presence is taken as a sign of how low Antony's fortunes have now
fallen. The schoolmaster as messenger reports that Antony
wishes to live in Egypt or else live 'a private man in Athens'.
Cleopatra wishes that her heirs may inherit her kingdom. Caesar
will not listen to Antony's request but will agree to Cleopatra's
provided that she exile Antony from Egypt or kill him. When the
schoolmaster has left, Caesar tells Thidias to try to win Cleopatra
from Antony and spy on Antony's activities. Thidias is given a
free hand as to how he proceeds.

Commentary

Caesar in control reveals himself as manipulative and intelligent.
Motivated by revenge he shows no mercy towards Antony and
clearly has other things in mind for Cleopatra. Note the rich use
of imagery, from a ruined bird deprived of a feather, to 'the
morn-dew on the myrtle-leaf', contrasted against Caesar's 'grand
sea'.

pluck'd i.e. stripped of his feathers.
pinion Feather.
circle The crown.
Now . . . grace i.e. Caesar is the victor and in control. The image is
taken from Elizabethan tennis where a point was gained by the ball
being hit into the opponent's 'hazard' – a wall hole or gallery.
Of audience . . . fail i.e. she'll obtain a meeting with me and get her
wishes.
Bring him through the bands Give him safe conduct through the
troops.
add more . . . offers The probable meaning is that he'll offer Cleopatra
more than has been suggested.
women . . . vestal Women are not even at the best of times strong-
minded, but necessity will break even the vows of the purest vestal virgin.
vestal A life of chastity dedicated to the goddess Vesta – the virgin.
Caesar's line is not without irony. Cleopatra is no 'vestal'!
cunning Skill.
Make thine . . . edict Make your own laws and regulations: name your
own reward.

becomes his flaw Acknowledge the breaches in honour (i.e. how Antony behaved at Actium).

his very action . . . moves i.e. make an assessment of what his real motives are.

Act III Scene 13

Enobarbus is questioned by Cleopatra about what to do and she asks if she is to blame. Enobarbus apportions the blame to Antony, who has allowed his reason to be controlled by his emotions. The schoolmaster ambassador has arrived. Antony sends him back to Caesar, challenging him to a duel which provokes Enobarbus in an aside to wonder at Antony's loss of reason. Caesar must be aware that Antony is a skilful swordsman. Thidias, Caesar's ambassador, arrives with a message for Cleopatra from Caesar, saying that he knows she only loves Antony out of fear. She replies that her honour has been conquered, not defeated; she accepts Caesar's victory and places her fate in his hands.

As Thidias is kissing Cleopatra's hand in farewell, Antony and Enobarbus enter. An enraged Antony orders Thidias to be whipped. He loses his self-control and in a jealous rage turns on Cleopatra, accusing her of various infidelities. A whipped Thidias returns, and Antony revels in humiliating him and, implicitly, his master Caesar, to whom Thidias is told to return and report what has happened.

Antony indulges in a bout of self-pity. Cleopatra, realizing that he isn't himself, indulges in self-accusations. Antony, passion cooled, is reconciled with Cleopatra, and makes preparations for another fight with Caesar's armies. He calls for one final night of mutual revelry. Cleopatra reveals that it is her birthday, which at least she is going to enjoy. Alone on stage, Enobarbus again says that Antony's reason has left him, and that he will 'seek some way to leave' Antony.

Commentary

This scene embodies loss of control and reason and the consequences. Antony's confidence in himself as a man of authority, as a military commander and as a lover, has been eroded. He acts out of jealous frenzy in having Thidias whipped. His lack of trust is shown in his mistaking Thidias's and Cleopatra's seemingly elaborate diplomatic exchange of niceties for genuine feeling. Thidias is Caesar's representative. Cleopatra is being conciliatory and safeguarding her future. Shakespeare's genius in the presentation of the complexity of human emotions further exhibits itself when the catalogue of charges Antony throws at Cleopatra contains elements of the truth. She was for instance 'a fragment/Of Gnaeus Pompey's'.

The tide of emotional fury ebbing and flowing dominates the scene. There are many prefiguring images in this scene of death, blood and destruction. Hunting and hawking metaphors – Antony 'will appear in blood', 'The dove' (Antony) 'will peck the estridge' (the goshawk Caesar) – vie with metaphors of pestilence and plague. If Cleopatra has been 'Cold-hearted toward' Antony then 'the flies and gnats of Nile' will devour her soldiers.

The depth of psychological insight into jealousy and rage in this scene is suggested by the great early nineteenth century literary critic Hazlitt, who comments that Antony suspects Thidias to be Caesar's proxy i.e. standing for Caesar himself!

Think, and die i.e. implying a dwelling upon loss bringing about utter depression and then death.

his will His passions. His passions have become greater than his reasoning power.

several ranges Separate ranks or lines of troops.

affection Passion.

nick'd Got the better of; cut short, curtailed.

mered question The reason for the dispute, the reason why one half of the world is opposed to the other half.

course Chase. A hunting term.

ministers Servants.

gay comparisons i.e. external finery and show (e.g. 'coin', 'ships', 'legions').

Unstate his happiness . . . sworder Forsake his happiness, put on a stage performance to fight a prize-winning swordsman. Enobarbus is being sarcastic.

A parcel of In keeping with, a reflection of.

things outward . . . alike External events so influence a man's inner judgement that both decline in a similar manner.

that he . . . emptiness! Having experienced all the exigences of fortune, Caesar at the height of his fortunes will place himself on equal terms with Antony, who will be at the nadir of his.

no more ceremony The servant's demeanour, without any polite preliminaries, represents the way in which Cleopatra's power has declined and Caesar's risen.

blown rose i.e. Cleopatra, who is no longer young like Caesar.

to square To quarrel. Enobarbus is addressing the audience in an aside.

He needs as many . . . not us Unless he has as many friends as Caesar he has no need of us for his case is hopeless.

Whose he is . . . Caesar's A confession of where true power now lies, i.e. with Caesar.

he is Caesar i.e. he will treat you with chivalry.

He knows . . . fear'd him Thidias cleverly is providing Cleopatra with an excuse if she wishes to use one.

But conquer'd merely Overcome by force or by Antony's persistent love and conquest. Cleopatra's answer is diplomatically ambiguous. She yields nothing.

art so leaky i.e. wanton, unreliable.

shroud Protection; a possible reference to Antony's funeral covering.

universal landlord Ruler of the Universe.

What's your name? Cleopatra seems interested in Thidias in his non-diplomatic role.

in deputation On my behalf.

Wisdom and . . . it If a wise person has the courage to remain wise then all will be well.

lay . . . hand i.e. kiss your hand.

Your Caesar's father . . . rain'd kisses Cleopatra is acting in her usual complex manner. She may (a) be engaged in a flirtation with Thidias on a personal level, and with Thidias as Caesar's representative; (b) indulging in erotic memories concerning a past love affair; (c) recalling past moments of power; (d) stalling for time until Antony appears.

thou Meant contemptuously. Antony has caught him in a compromising position.

fullest man The man with the most authority.

Approach there Addressed to Antony's attendants.

kite The kite is a bird of prey, so hardly a compliment to Cleopatra.

unto a muss Running into a scramble – as children after a ball or nuts.

lion's whelp A young lion, i.e. Caesar.

an old one dying i.e. Antony.

tributaries Dependant kings.

what's her . . . Cleopatra? Marvellous contempt: Cleopatra is no longer what she was.

cringe Screw up.

Forborne . . . race Refrained from 'the getting' of legitimate children.

looks on feeders Looks with favours on servants.

boggler Word implying literally ' "a fumbler": hence, an adulteress, or perhaps a strumpet' (Partridge, *Shakespeare's Bawdy*, p.68).

seel our eyes Close our eyes. The metaphor is from falconry where the young hawk's eyelids are sewn up or sealed in order to accustom it to using a hood.

morsel i.e. as one of Julius Caesar's leavings: Cleopatra has described herself as 'A morsel for a monarch' (I, 5).

trencher Wooden plate.

Gnaeus Pompey See note, I,2, on 'Pompey the Great' p.27; also note I, 5, 'Great Pompey' on p.33.

Unregister'd in vulgar fame Unknown to the common people.

quit Reward.

And plighter of high hearts! By which the hearts of the nobility pledged themselves, i.e. by the kissing of hands.

hill of Basan A reference to Psalm lxviii,15: 'The hill of God is as the hill of Bashan; an high hill as the hill of Bashan'. It was famous for its rich pastures, fat bulls and oak forests. It was situated east of the river Jordan and south of Mount Hermon.

horned herd Antony is assuming he is a cuckold and thinking of the imaginary horns of the cuckold.

yare Skilful and speedy.

fever thee Make you shake as though suffering with fever. Antony's use of second person singular throughout this speech expresses his contempt.

entertainment Treatment.

orbs Spheres.

shot their fire . . . hell A powerful image of cosmic disruption. cf. Revelations ix,1–2: 'I saw a star fall from heaven unto the earth: and to him was given the key of the bottomless pit/And he opened the bottomless pit; and there arose a smoke out of the pit, as the smoke of a great furnace.'

Hipparchus . . . enfranched The first of Antony's men to desert to Caesar. He was a freed slave.

quit Gain revenge on.

one that . . . points i.e. Caesar's servant, who laces up clothes ('points' were laces on clothes).

Not know me yet? (a) Antony is still jumping to conclusions (b) is so preoccupied with his grief and anger that he hasn't yet noticed her.

determines Melts (and releases its poison). The image of the universe pelted with poisoned hailstones is an effective one, especially as their source would be Cleopatra's 'cold heart'. The contrast is with her passionate self which has become hardened and poisonous.

memory Memorials, i.e. her children.

discandying Melting.

pelleted The hail frozen into pellets.

most sea-like i.e. his navy is ship-shape.

in blood The metaphor is from hunting and refers to a stag in excellent condition. Antony means either he'll return bloodstained after experiencing a fierce fight; or will return in good condition.

earn our chronicle Place in history.

men did . . . for jests I spared lives in return for a joke.

poor i.e. without too much expense.

since my lord . . . Cleopatra A brief restoration and return to former glories and activities.

noble captains With the change in mood, 'sad captains' have become 'noble ones'.

force the wine . . . scars An expressive image suggesting forced jollity and pain.

outstare the lightning An image of Antony defying nature.

frightened out of fear i.e. fear no longer holds any fears.
The dove . . . estridge The estridge is the goshawk (a bird of prey).
  The realist Enobarbus identifies Antony with the dove associated with
  Venus (goddess of love and beauty) and Caesar with the goshawk.
diminution in our . . . heart i.e. as he loses his intelligence his courage
  returns.
when valour preys . . . with i.e. Antony is fighting without using his
  head. Mere courage is not enough.

Revision questions on Act III

1 What happens at Actium? Assess the ways in which the events
are conveyed in Act III.
2 Compare and contrast the function and treatment of the two
ambassadors or messengers in the Act.
3 Why is Enobarbus still with Antony at the end of the Act?
4 'This Act is concerned with contrasting moods based on the
turns of the wheel of fortune.' Discuss with reference to both
Antony and Cleopatra.
5 Show the ways in which the young Caesar displays his astute-
ness in this Act.

Act IV Scene 1

Caesar reads Antony's letter and is angered by his threats,
especially as they lack substance. Maecenas, Caesar's lieutenant,
ridicules Antony's challenge to single combat and urges Caesar
to take advantage of Antony's distraught condition. Caesar,
aware that the forthcoming battle will prove to be a decisive one,
intends to satisfy his army. He prepares a feast and refers to the
numbers of Antony's former soldiers who have come over to his
side.

Commentary

Octavius shows that he is sensitive to criticism. His anger, though
kept in check, will result at the conclusion of the play in his hard
attitude to Antony. Caesar, a much younger man, is trying to
show that he acts maturely, which is why Antony's calling him a
'boy' and whipping his messenger (a replacement for Caesar) so
incenses him. Antony is insulting his masculinity and maturity.
Increasingly Antony is blustering without the 'power' to 'beat'
Caesar 'out of Egypt'. Metaphors from the hunt, references to
Antony as 'the old ruffian' prepare the audience for Antony's

destruction. He too as a stag or boar is being 'hunted/Even to falling'.

he's hunted . . . falling A metaphor from hunting a stag or a boar.
Make boot of his distraction Take advantage of his (Antony's) insanity.
Made good guard The metaphor is from swordsmanship: the angry man is unable to present a good guard.
best heads Those in command.
store Enough resources.
waste Expense. Note the contrast between Caesar's 'store', his careful nurturing of resources and Antony's 'waste', his superfluity.

Act IV Scene 2

Caesar's reply that he will not fight Antony in single combat forces Antony to prepare for the next day's decisive battle. Antony bids a sad farewell to his followers, reminds them of former glories, and suggests that their supper will prove to be their last, for tomorrow they will have another master. Enobarbus warns Antony that he is fostering depression. Antony, in an effort to restore spirits, tells his attendants that he doesn't mean what he says and that he'll join them in supper to 'drown considerations'.

Commentary

A humbled rather than a distraught Antony is seen. He is generous to his followers. Unlike Caesar, he'll join them in supper. Antony is aware that the morning will witness the final decisive battle and that his servants will probably have a new master. There is interesting use of metaphor and powerful lines. Enobarbus, in an aside to an almost silent Cleopatra, tells her of Antony's farewell to his servants, ' 'Tis one of those odd tricks which sorrow shoots/Out of the mind.' The alliteration, arrow imagery, and suggestion of mental disorientation effectively combine together. Antony's comment that his followers the next day may see him 'A mangled shadow' joins together an image of destruction with one of physical change into a 'shadow'. And the cynical Enobarbus, in an effort to shut off powerful sentimental emotions – tears of sadness – is 'an ass', he is 'onion-ey'd'.

bathe my . . . live again A reference to an old belief that to bathe in blood restored youth. Antony in order to regain lost honour will slaughter his enemies in battle.

Woo't Wilt – a contracted form of 'wouldst thou'.

'Take all' A gambling term meaning 'let the winner take all'. Notice it is
  Enobarbus who says this line – he is only too aware of how much of a
  gamble the whole business is. Enobarbus's reference to 'I'll strike'
  might be an ironic commentary on Antony's activities at Actium.
  There he 'struck' his sails, left the scene of battle, and went to
  Cleopatra. Enobarbus is shortly to forsake Antony.

clapp'd up together Joined together. Also sense of imprisonment.
  Their destinies are linked.

Scant Begrudge.

or if i.e. if you do see me again it will be as . . . .

yield Reward.

onion-eyed cf. I, 2 'the tears live in an onion that should water this
  sorrow'. Here Enobarbus's tears are genuine.

take me Bewitch me. Perhaps 'the witch' is an ironic reference to
  Cleopatra, who has cast a spell on Antony!

Grace grow . . . drops fall i.e. may only good (gentleness and kindness)
  arise from your tears. There is a pun on 'grace' referring to the herb
  of grace – rue.

consideration Melancholy sad thoughts.

Act IV Scene 3

A conversation between three soldiers on duty. Rumours of
strange noises are unconfirmed; however they agree that if the
navy succeeds and the army fights well victory will be theirs.
Music is heard. A soldier regards the noise as a good omen,
another a bad omen as the sounds represent the spirit of Hercules 'whom Antony lov'd' leaving him. The soldiers attempt to
track down the source of the music.

Commentary

A brief scene concentrating on atmosphere and superstition.
The brief speeches, short questions and answers, physical pacing
to and fro across the stage, suggest restlessness, unease and
foreboding. The image of 'the god Hercules, whom Antony
lov'd' which 'Now leaves him' is that of Antony's favourite pro-
tective god deserting him, and serves as an anticipatory image.
Antony is shortly to die. The scene presents ordinary soldiers
and their activities rather than the rulers of empires. It also
introduces the element of the superstitions associated with
mysterious sounds and omens, frequently used by Shakespeare
to prepare for dramatic or tragic events.

landmen will stand up Our soldiers will stand up to the enemy.
purpose Strength and absolution.
hautboys Oboes.
we have quarter As far as we are allowed (by our sentry duty).
how it will give off How it will end.

Act IV Scene 4

Cleopatra helps Antony put on his armour. Her assistance is not entirely successful. A soldier arrives to tell Antony that he is expected for the battle. Trumpets sound; he tells his men that the day is a 'fair' one, and as a soldier takes leave of Cleopatra. She retires to her chamber with the thought that if only Antony and Caesar 'might/Determine this great war in single fight!' all would be well.

Commentary

Antony is in his soldier's role as a man of duty and responsibility. Cleopatra is her natural sensuous self.

mine armour, Eros Remember that Eros is the Greek god of love as well as being literally Antony's servant, and that 'armour' is a pun on both military uniform and passion.
chuck Chick (a term of endearment).
thine iron That armour you have for me.
armourer Sustenance, strength.
false, false; this, this Probably Cleopatra has (intentionally or otherwise) put the armour on Antony incorrectly. Antony shows her the correct way to do so. Stage actions make this clear. There is some opportunity for body language between them. 'False, false, this, this' literally means 'wrong, that's not the right way to do it, this is'.
dafft Take it off.
squire Knight's attendant; close personal attendant.
tight Skilled, apt.
royal occupation i.e. warfare, the business of monarchs.
workman Expert.
charge Order.
riveted trim Armour.
port Gate.
well blown A reference to the trumpets, to the sounds of battle.
well said i.e. well done.
to stand/On more mechanic compliment To stand on formal compliments and dignity.

Act IV Scene 5

A soldier greets Antony, who admits his mistake in not engaging in a land battle at Actium. The soldier tells him that Enobarbus has gone over to Caesar. Antony generously sends Enobarbus his treasures, 'gentle adieus, and greetings' and regrets that his 'fortunes have/Corrupted honest men'!

Commentary

This shows a magnanimous Antony, who admits his errors in not heeding the soldier's advice to fight by land and doesn't treat Enobarbus meanly in spite of his defection. Indeed Antony blames himself. Large numbers of his troops have also left him; however, his feelings are not for them, or necessarily for his own sorry plight, but for Enobarbus and his welfare.

happy Lucky.
Would. . . land! This soldier seems to be the one who unsuccessfully attempted to persuade Antony to fight by land at Actium.
Is he gone? Antony refuses to believe the news.
do it Eros is probably astonished at Antony's generous reaction.
subscribe Sign it.

Act IV Scene 6

At Caesar's camp, where he gives orders for the battle to commence and orders that Antony be captured alive. He also commands that the deserters from Antony's side be placed in the front lines. Enobarbus, hearing these instructions, regrets his defection. A soldier appears to tell him that Antony has sent over Enobarbus's possessions and added more to them. Enobarbus is overcome with remorse and plans suicide.

Commentary

A scene of contrasts, short but revealing. Caesar clearly is in command giving precise orders indicating that he wishes to humiliate Antony by taking him alive. Further, we are told that he has consistently shown no tolerance towards deserters. The focus after the initial ten lines is upon Enobarbus and the absent Antony. Enobarbus already regrets his move. Antony's generosity incenses him even more. Perhaps Antony, aware of his close friend's weaknesses, knew that a 'bounty overplus' would be the straw to break him. On the other hand, the extra goods and his decision to allow Enobarbus his property probably sprang from Antony's generosity. Even an enemy soldier is impressed by Antony's action: 'Your emperor,' he tells Enobarbus, 'continues still a Jove.' Previously we have witnessed Antony's mental distraction. Now Enobarbus's despair and sense of total humiliation are revealed in imagery describing 'blows' to the heart.

The time...is near Dramatic irony. The final battle between Antony and Caesar was not 'the war to end all wars'!

three-nook'd i.e. the divisions of the Roman Empire. But Lepidus is dead, so could refer to the sea, the sky and the land, or to Europe, Africa and Asia.

bear the olive i.e. live peacefully. The olive branch is the Roman emblem for peace.

charge Order.

Alexas...Antony Notice that Enobarbus's emphasis is on Alexas's desertion.

dissuade Persuade.

fell away Deserted.

have entertainment...trust Are taken into Caesar's service but not in positions of responsibility.

His bounty overplus With an additional bonus (an extra gift).

saf'd...host Give safe-conduct to the bringer through our army lines.

Jove i.e. in his generosity.

most i.e. more than anyone.

blows Swells with grief; pains and saddens.

If swift thought i.e. melancholy, depressing ideas filling my mind.

foul'st i.e. dirtiest ditch.

My latter part of life My final hours.

Act IV Scene 7

Different views of the battle. Agrippa indicates that Caesar's forces are under pressure. Scarus, on the other hand, although wounded, reports that things are going well for Antony's forces.

Commentary

The first of six scenes presenting differing viewpoints of the battle. As with the individual combatants, it is difficult to obtain an overall impression of events. Fortunes ebb and flow. Note the ferocity of the fighting indicated by Scarus's wound and the pugnacious nature of his references; he will 'score' the 'backs' of his enemies.

has work Is preoccupied with tough fighting.
  our oppression The enemy's pressure (i.e. Antony's armies).
clouts Bandages.
H Pronounced the same as 'ache'. A curious moment for Scarus to
  indulge in word-play, especially as he is seriously wounded.
bench-holes The holes in the lavatory benches.
scotches Slashes.
score Mark, brand. Clearly no leniency was shown by either side in
  battle.
snatch A metaphor from hunting, when the hound seized the hare.
runner Runaway.
spritely Cheerful.
halt Limp.

Act IV Scene 8

Antony sends a messenger to Cleopatra with victory news. He
thanks his troops for heroic efforts and predicts victory the next
day. Cleopatra arrives. They mutually praise one another and
Scarus is personally recommended to Cleopatra for bravery.
Together Antony and Cleopatra will celebrate.

Commentary

Antony is in command of the situation and his men. Metaphors
of war mingle with those of sensuality. The scene is pervaded by
an underlying irony, for Antony's joy is to prove short-lived. His
lines: 'drink carouses to the next day's fate,/Which promises
royal peril' in fact becomes a toast to his own destruction and
'royal peril' rather than Caesar's.

gests Deeds, achievements.
Each man's like mine i.e. as if the battle has been their personal
  concern.
shown all Hectors All shown yourselves to be as valiant as Hector (the
  great Trojan hero during the Greek siege of Troy).
clip Embrace.
great fairy i.e. Cleopatra, phrase suggesting enchantress, bringer of
  good fortune.
proof of harness i.e. my armour which is impenetrable.
virtue Bravery.
great snare i.e. war, in the sense of entrapment.
this man i.e. Scarus.
Commend unto . . . warrior An interesting contrast with Antony's
  reaction to the discovery of Thidias kissing Cleopatra's hand.
had . . . shape In human form, killed.

carbuncled A gem of a deep red colouring.
targets Shields.
 owe Own.
carouses Toasts.
royal peril Peril to Caesar.
tabourines Side-drums.

Act IV Scene 9

A sentry and watchman talk in Caesar's camp. They hear sounds of a man in torment. This is Enobarbus who, heart-broken with guilt and remorse, dies. The drum sounds for the coming battle as his body is taken to the guardroom.

Commentary

Enobarbus's death from a broken heart is rendered even more moving by his isolation, remorse, and the fact that his final words are 'O Antony! O Antony!'. The repetition of the name of the leader he has deserted, with the double 'O' sounds, adds to the pathos. His final speeches combine images of melancholic depression with conceits revolving round psychological and material conditions of hardness. Alliteration and run-on-line effectively juxtapose with image in his 'Throw my heart/Against the flint and hardness of my fault'. As he dies and literally disintegrates so the line lengths break down and become shorter and shorter.

Enobarbus's body is accorded some dignity by being borne 'To th' court of guard' for 'he is of note'. Notice also how such a brief scene of just over 30 lines, with an acting time of probably less than five stage minutes, conveys the passage of time. The first soldier, hearing the drums calling men to war, remarks that 'our hour/Is fully out'. This scene is placed between Antony's anticipation of victory and his ensuing conversation with Scarus. Of course the soldier's comment has a double meaning: the lives of many will be 'fully out' before the sun sets again.

shrewd Bad.
O sovereign . . . melancholy i.e. the moon, to whose changes deep depression was attributed.
disponge i.e. drip, as if squeezed from a sponge.
a very rebel to my will i.e. which continues in spite of my desire for death.
flint and . . . fault Notice the yoking together of the metaphorical 'flint'

and its quality of 'hardness' – an example of a conceit (a joining together of often dissimilar images).

Which being . . . powder In depressive grief the heart lost blood at each sigh. So Enobarbus's heart 'will break to powder' when the enormity of his fault becomes apparent.

rank me in register Record me.

A master-leaver An apprentice who has run away from his master. An apprentice would be trained by a master-workman; Enobarbus has become an expert at leaving his master, Antony.

raught Reached.

Demurely Firmly but quietly so as not to wake the enemy.

Act IV Scene 10

Antony confers with Scarus. Caesar has prepared for a naval battle. Antony is prepared on land and sea. He goes to the hills near the city to discover what is happening.

Commentary

A short sharp perspective on the coming battle. Preparations are made, and Antony is acting rationally.

For both i.e. for both land and sea battles.
I would . . . there too i.e. in the four elements: water, earth, fire, air.
appointment Preparation.

Act IV Scene 11

Caesar instructs his forces to wait while Antony puts his best men into a naval confrontation. Caesar's men will hold their ground in the valleys.

Commentary

A different perspective on proceedings, this time from Caesar's point of view. The military and strategic battle of wits continues.

forth Gone forth.
vales The valleys. Note that Caesar avoids engaging Antony in the hills.
And hold . . . advantage i.e. secure the strongest position we can.

Act IV Scene 12

Antony finds a high observation point to watch the battle. Scarus notes that the fortune tellers have been negative about Antony's chances. Antony re-enters with the news that he has been betrayed. His fleet has surrendered. He assumes that Cleopatra has deserted him, and when she appears he vents his rage on her and threatens to kill her on the spot. She does not stay. He calls upon Hercules to give him the strength to take his own life and to gain revenge on Cleopatra.

Commentary

This is the culmination of six scenes presenting differing viewpoints of the battle's shifting fortunes. In the initial scenes Antony is confident of victory, and he is re-united with Cleopatra. Enobarbus deserts and dies, Antony's fortunes turn. Scenes 10 and 11 show brief shifting perspectives, and this scene brings his fortunes to their lowest point.

Antony's bitterness towards Cleopatra (based on the flimsiest of evidence, since he doesn't know for sure that she has gone over to Caesar) is related to his loss of power, sense of impotence and sexual jealousy. He has lost to a younger man Caesar; Cleopatra has gone over to Caesar.

The scene is full of imagery extending from the solitary pine of the opening line, Antony's vision of Cleopatra as a 'Triple-turn'd whore', the vision of fawning dogs, the tree ruined by its bark being removed, to the culminating vision of self-destruction and fire. The invocation of Hercules ironically suggests a strength which has now gone from Antony, draws upon Antony's obsession with (Cleopatra's) infidelity (Hercules's wife was unfaithful), the sacrifice of the innocents (Lichas the servant perhaps representing the innocent soldiers and sailors who have died, or perhaps Enobarbus). This is a powerful, destructive account.

yond pine . . . all A specific detail helping to locate the setting, also ironic – Antony's power and possessions have been reduced to a pine tree.

Swallows have . . . their nests An image prefiguring disaster. The source is North's Plutarch: 'there chaunced a marvelous ill signe. Swallowes had bred under the poope of her shippe, and there came others after them that drave away the first, and plucked downe their neasts.'

augurers Those who interpret omens.

fretted Worn away.

Of what . . . has not Notice the way the line is balanced to convey the alternation of fortune.

Triple-turn'd whore Again powerful language, three words convey Antony's contempt. He is referring to Cleopatra's activities with Julius Caesar; Pompey; Antony; and perhaps in the future, Caesar.

my heart Real emotions.

my charm i.e. Cleopatra, who has bewitched me. Observe the number of personal pronouns used at this point of the speech. Antony is again self-absorbed. The battle has for the moment been forgotten: his obsession is again with himself and Cleopatra.

spaniel'd me . . . i.e. fawned on me like spaniels. The image is full of contempt. (It is doubtful whether Romans or Egyptians had spaniels.)

discandy Melt the sugar.

pine i.e. himself rather than the actual pine of the opening line of the scene.

bark'd Stripped bare.

grave charm Deadly witch.

eye . . . my wars At whose mere glance my wars were started.

beck'd Beckoned.

crownet i.e. the crown of my happiness, my chief delight.

right Proper.

at fast and loose i.e. a game of deception in which a gambler believes incorrectly that knots in string are real ones.

Avaunt! Word used to get rid of witches.

blemish Caesar's triumph i.e. I'll kill you.

spot Blemish, disgrace, also with the sense of staining a woman's honour.

poor'st diminutives, for dolts For the delight of weaklings.

Patient Long suffering.

prepared Sharpened.

The shirt of Nessus Nessus the centaur was killed by Hercules with a poisoned arrow. He had attempted to run away with Hercules's wife Deianira. As he died he dipped the shirt in his poisoned blood and assured Deianira that if Hercules's love for her faded the shirt would restore it. Deianira sent the shirt to Hercules via a young messenger Lichas. Hercules put the poisoned shirt on and was burnt alive. In his agony he seized the innocent Lichas and hurled him into the ocean.

Alcides A descendant of Alceus, the grandfather of Hercules.

those hands . . . heaviest club The hands of Hercules.

Subdue . . . self Destroy myself.

Act IV Scene 13

Back at her palace a frantic Cleopatra seeks help. Charmian advises her to lock herself in the tomb and to send word to

Antony that she is dead. Cleopatra tells Mardian to give Antony the message, to add that the word 'Antony' is on her lips when she dies, and to let her know how he received the news.

Commentary

Cleopatra is frantic; her usual perceptive insight seems to have deserted her. She misjudges Antony's mood and situation with tragic consequences. She relies upon her attendants rather than on herself to make decisions. Notice how she appeals to the memory of others who believed themselves to be wronged and acted from impulse – Telamon and Diana. Telamon could well be Antony, Diana, the revengeful goddess, Cleopatra.

more mad . . . Telamon Ajax of Telamon, who went mad when Odysseus rather than he received the shield of Achilles awarded to the bravest of the Greeks who survived the Trojan war.
boar of Thessaly A destructive boar was sent by Diana to ravage Calydon in ancient Greece. Oeneus, the king, had refused to offer sacrifices to her.
emboss'd Totally exhausted (as a hunted animal at bay).
monument Tomb.

Act IV Scene 14

Antony talks with Eros about his impending death. He blames Cleopatra for his undoing and contemplates suicide. Mardian, Cleopatra's messenger, arrives with the false information that she has died. This news hardens Antony's resolution to die. He asks Eros to kill him, but Eros kills himself instead. Antony, full of remorse and a sense of his own cowardice, tries to kill himself by falling on his sword. Lying wounded, he is found by two guards, who refuse his request to kill him. Diomedes appears. Cleopatra has had a premonition concerning the consequences of her false report. She has sent Diomedes to tell Antony the truth. Antony requests that as a final service his guard carry him to Cleopatra.

Commentary

There is fine poetic imagery in this scene. Antony's 'Sometime we see a cloud that's dragonish' speech provoked Hazlitt to write that 'The splendour of the imagery, the semblance of reality, the lofty range of picturesque objects hanging over the world, their evanescent nature, the total uncertainty of what is left behind, are just like the mouldering scenes of human greatness.'

Antony decides on suicide when he feels totally forsaken. All he desires is to 'o'ertake thee Cleopatra, and/Weep for my pardon'. However, Eros stoically kills himself rather than Antony. It is ironic that Antony is unable to kill himself properly – his fortune will not allow him to make a clean job of it. After he has wounded himself he learns that Cleopatra is still alive, and the path is cleared for a final meeting between the two in this life rather than, as he has hoped, in the next. His aborted suicide demonstrates that Antony, a person who has controlled empires, no longer controls his own fate. Antony must live on a little longer. The Roman stoical values of heroic death (expressed in Eros's death and Brutus's in *Julius Caesar*) are not for Antony.

Eros . . . me i.e. Antony has lost his confidence, he isn't too sure that he exists any more.

dragonish i.e. shaped like a dragon.

pendent Overhanging.

black vesper's pageants i.e. the signs in the clouds indicating the coming of evening. This is the only instance in Shakespeare of the use of the word 'vesper' (evening): 'pageants' are displays.

a thought i.e. the speed of thought.

rack dislimns Clouds disintegrate.

Yet cannot hold . . . shape i.e. soon I shall stop being what I am.

knave Servant (boy).

moe More.

Pack'd cards with Caesar Shuffled the cards in Caesar's favour.

and . . . triumph By cheating at cards betrayed me so that my glory has become my enemy's triumph. Note also that 'triumph' echoes 'trump' in cards. Antony is saying that Cleopatra's activities have allowed Caesar to 'trump' him.

paid but once . . . discharged A play on 'debt', 'death', and 'discharged' – the debt has been paid.

unto thy hand Waiting for you as you required.

name so buried in her Your name was on her lips unexpressed as she died.

Unarm, Eros Antony now asks Eros to remove the armour which he had put on him (see Scene 4).

The seven-fold shield of Ajax A Greek hero at Troy, Ajax had a brass shield backed with seven layers of ox-hide.

battery i.e. the blows against my heart.

once i.e. for once.

continent The physical frame, the body, containing you.

bruised pieces Battered pieces of armour.

Weep for my pardon Antony thinks (mistakenly) that his words have caused Cleopatra's death.

length i.e. the rest of my life.

torch i.e. the light of life. Antony may be referring to Cleopatra, or to himself and his own life.

Mars what it does Is wasted.

very force . . . strength i.e. is useless.

seal . . . done The metaphor is taken from sealing a document such as a will – everything is brought to an end.

Where . . . flowers i.e. in the Elysium fields of Greek paradise.

sprightly port Spirited appearance.

Dido, and her Aeneas Ironic; here Antony reconciles Dido and Aeneas, but in Virgil's *Aeneid* Dido deserted her lover Aeneas in Hades to return to her husband.

shall want troops Lack admirers, i.e. all the ghosts (spirits) will come over to Antony and Cleopatra: 'troops' is a pun on the soldiers who in life deserted Antony.

And all the haunt be ours i.e. we will be the main attraction: 'haunt' is the place haunted by ghosts.

Quarter'd the world Took over the world.

o'er green Neptune's back . . . cities So covered the seas with ships that they were transformed into cities. An impressive image of man's power to transform nature.

exigent Need.

inevitable prosecution Pursuit from which escape is impossible.

Parthian darts Arrows used by the Parthians whom Antony had been unable to defeat.

window'd Placed at a window.

pleach'd arms Folded arms.

corrigible neck Forced to submit to others' commands.

branded . . . ensued i.e. humiliated Antony, who followed him as a slave.

wound . . . cur'd Notice the paradox between 'wound' and 'cured', revealing Antony's turmoil.

precedent Previous.

accidents unpurpos'd i.e. without purpose.

Wherein . . . world lies Which the whole world worships.

why For which.

The star is fall'n Notice the astronomical image with its Biblical echoes, cf. Revelation, viii, 10: 'And the third angel sounded, and there fell a great star from heaven.'

time is . . . period Time itself stands still.

Shall enter me with him i.e. show me in a favourable light. Another example of how in moments of dramatic tension Shakespeare demonstrates human ingenuity. Decretas tries to take advantage of the situation.

dispos'd with Come to an agreement with.

purg'd Driven away.

Act IV Scene 15

A severely wounded Antony is brought to the monument where Cleopatra is in hiding with her handmaidens. Cleopatra, unable to leave the monument out of fear of capture by Caesar's troops, pulls Antony into the monument, helped by her maidens. She pleads with him to clear her name. Antony advises her to make peace with Caesar, but Cleopatra declares that she'll never trust Caesar. Antony tells her to remember his greatness, and Cleopatra faints when he dies. For her life is no longer worth living. She tells Charmian and Iras that they will bury Antony and then copy the Romans by committing suicide.

Commentary

This is a scene of searing rhetoric and great speeches. For instance, Cleopatra's speech beginning 'Noblest of men, woo't die?' eventually reduces the world to insignificance now that Antony 'the crown o' the earth' is gone.

Although Cleopatra refuses to place her own self at risk and refuses to leave the monument to see the dying Antony, her femininity and true love for him emerge in this scene. She scorns his noble advice to her to make peace with Caesar, and is shattered by his death. Antony's death reconciles the two and reveals the extent of their love for each other. Cleopatra will follow him to the grave.

There is some irony in the theatricality of the scene, which probably takes place on the upper stage where Antony is hauled presumably by a sling. The move from a lower stage level to an upper level is a reflection of Antony's continual reaching out for Cleopatra. Even in death he has to go to her, rather than have her going to him. The movement of the wounded dying body in a sling hardly adds to Antony's dignity, yet his death, and its reception, is not without honour. This feeling of decorum is largely created by Cleopatra's poetry and her expression of genuine sentiment, in addition to Antony's restrained acceptance of death.

our size of . . . makes it The extent of our sorrow must be as great as the event which caused it.

Not Caesar's valour . . . itself Antony assures Cleopatra that Caesar hasn't defeated him: his wound has been self inflicted. Antony still has some pride.

importune death awhile i.e. ask death not to come too quickly.

thousand kisses . . . lips Note the poetic contrast, 'many thousand' becomes 'the poor last'.

I dare not i.e. leave her hiding place in the monument.

brooch'd Celebrated, ornamented (as with a brooch).

still conclusion Quiet judgement (implying disapproval).

Demuring upon Gazing down at (in negative judgement).

There's sport indeed! Rather an ironic remark, but Cleopatra is probably referring to the exertion of pulling Antony up, for he is heavy and her heaviness of heart makes the task the more difficult.

Mercury The 'strong-wing'd' messenger of the Roman gods.

Wishers were ever fools i.e. those who waste time wishing always were fools. Note the alliterative 'w' and 'e' sounds adding to the pithy appropriateness of the comment.

Quicken Bring to life.

heavy sight Sorry sight.

so high So loudly.

huswife i.e. hussy – also a jibe at false women.

Fortune break her wheel Fortune was personified in the form of a blind goddess with a wheel. When the turn of the wheel made man's fortunes low the goddess became a harlot, a 'hussy', a 'huswife'.

They do not go together Cleopatra suggests that in order to have safe guarantees from Caesar she'll have to sacrifice her honour.

Proculeius See V,1, Summary.

Valiantly vanquish'd Notice the length of the words, the repetition of sounds and the downward rhythmic effect.

can i.e. can function no longer.

woo't Will you.

I abide . . . than a sty? Notice the powerful internal rhyme effect of 'abide' culminating in the forceful 'sty'.

pole Star; military weapon; military standard bearer.

young boys . . . men Cleopatra conveys the sense of somebody so powerful having fallen that everyone else is reduced to the same level.

the odds i.e. the differences between Antony (who was far superior) and other men.

Beneath . . . moon A reference to the universe below the heavens. A remarkable image conveying the dullness of existence now that Antony has gone. Cleopatra suggests that the moon has no longer anything to see when it visits, and shines upon, the earth.

O quietness Cleopatra has fainted.

chares Chores. Note the repetitive alliterative 'm' sounds used to convey Cleopatra's sense of disgust and despair.

our jewel i.e. Antony.

sottish Foolish.

Our lamp is . . . out (a) Antony's life; (b) our life's course; (c) the source of our inspiration.

sirs Sometimes used in Shakespeare's time to address women.

after the high Roman fashion i.e. suicide was considered by the Romans (not necessarily by the Egyptians) an honourable course of action. The Stoic philosophers taught that suicide was preferable to dishonour, such as being led as a captive in triumph through Rome.

case Body.

Revision questions on Act IV

1 Compare and contrast Antony's changes of mood and fortune in Act IV.
2 Write an account of Cleopatra's activities in Act IV.
3 Show the ways in which the Act presents the activities and reactions of ordinary soldiers. What is their function in the play?
4 Write an analysis of the function of some of the imagery in this Act.
5 How is battle presented in this Act?

Act V Scene 1

Dolabella is told by Caesar to insist that Antony makes peace. Decretas arrives carrying his sword, with which Antony had tried to kill himself, and with the news that Antony is dead. Caesar laments the loss of 'my mate in empire' and 'is touched'. An Egyptian messenger from Cleopatra arrives in order to discover what Caesar wants Cleopatra to do. Caesar says that she will soon find out, but that he will be generous. Proculeius, the only one of Caesar's circle trusted by Cleopatra, is sent to reassure her. Caesar is worried that she may follow Antony and commit suicide. He wishes to lead her through Rome as a triumph to his victory. Dolabella is called for, but Caesar remembers he has been sent on another errand.

Commentary

The focus is on Caesar and his reactions to Antony's death. He is now the supreme ruler, the surviving triumvir, the only star in the constellations. Caesar's triumph has been the result of the destruction of others. His reactions to Antony's death are an honest tribute to his enemy. His death 'Is not a single doom, in the name lay/A moiety of the world'. It creates a power vacuum which will be filled by Caesar.

The scene presents contrasting reactions to Antony's death. Caesar's close friends Decretas and Agrippa echo his words. Maecenas, on the other hand, contrasts ironically Caesar's face with Antony's: 'When such a spacious mirror's set before him/He needs must see himself'. Maecenas balances Antony's negative and positive qualities: 'His taints and honours/Waged equal with him.' In the final scene of the play Cleopatra's passionate emotional reactions to Antony's death will emerge.

In a scene presenting imagery of disease, disorder, kingship, war, and the heavens, political considerations are also found. Caesar's attitude to Cleopatra is politically motivated. He has power, and wishes to use her as a symbol of his victory over Antony. At the end of the scene, alone on stage and in control of the Roman Empire, Caesar appears a troubled solitary figure, eclipsed by Antony's memory.

tell him, he . . . makes His attempt to delay the day of his surrender is pointless.

what art thou . . . to us? Decretas has managed to get through Caesar's bodyguards with a bloody sword. No wonder Caesar is surprised.

wore my life A metaphor from wearing a sword. Decretas says that he has given his life defeating Antony's enemies.

breaking Death; bringing the news.

crack Explosion, and remember the expression the 'crack of doom'. The line is interesting. The six words are nicely balanced by a caesura to convey the effect of 'crack' and the effect of the news on Caesar. The last two words almost rhyme and are onomatopoeiac.

The round world . . . dens Disorder and unnatural happenings took place the night before Julius Caesar was murdered. Traditionally, 'lions' are the kings of the beasts. In using the comparison Caesar is paying the dead Antony (who has become a lion) a tribute. **Single doom** means the death of one man, and **a moiety of** refers to half (the world). Note the repetition of the word 'world' and the repetitive 'o' sounds which has the effect of showing Caesar's grief and highlighting a greatness gone from the 'world'.

lend i.e. give.

Splitted . . . sword Note the effective balancing caesura separating 'heart' from 'sword'.

steer humanity Guide people.

mirror Warning as well as example.

He needs must . . . himself i.e. Caesar will see himself in comparison with Antony.

followed Driven.

launch Lance, remove; i.e. Antony's weaknesses were diseases in the political body of Rome which had to be removed (cut away like a diseased part of the body).

declining day . . . thine Either (a) when my power came to an end (b) or observed your fall.

sovereign Valuable, powerful.

competitor Equal, rival.

In top . . . design In all our highest enterprises.

Where mine his . . . kindle He inspired me, my heart was inspired by his.

this i.e. to the point where one of us must die.

looks out of him i.e. reveals its urgency in his expression.

all she has . . . monument Cleopatra's power, her Empire, is now reduced to a monument.

ours i.e. servants, messengers.

quality of her passion Nature of her grief.

her life i.e. Cleopatra alive.

eternal i.e. would make my victory eternally memorable.

second Support.

hardly Unwittingly.

writings Communications with Antony.

Act V Scene 2

Proculeius arrives at the entrance to Cleopatra's monument with Caesar's surrender terms. He emphasizes Caesar's generosity if Cleopatra will submit to his authority. Gallus and soldiers enter the monument and seize Cleopatra from behind. She tries to kill herself, but is disarmed by Proculeius. She tells him that she would rather die than be led in triumph by Caesar. Dolabella enters and takes over from Proculeius. Cleopatra gives Dolabella an account of a dream she has had about Antony and praises him. She discovers from Dolabella the fate Caesar has in store for her. Then for the first time in the play she and Caesar meet. Cleopatra kneels before him, Caesar reassures her that no harm will come to her. Seleucus, her treasurer, after declaring that he has handed over Cleopatra's wealth, then reveals that a portion has been retained, and is driven from the stage by Cleopatra. Caesar allows her to retain the treasure and departs with reassuring words. When he leaves Cleopatra expresses scepticism about his intentions: 'He words me girls, he words me.'

Dolabella reappears and tells Cleopatra that in three days she'll be sent to Rome with her children. Cleopatra depicts a theatrical picture to Iras and Charmian of how they will be led in triumph before the Roman crowds. She sends for her 'best attires', 'crown and all', to prepare for suicide. A guard admits a clown carrying a fig basket in which are hidden poisonous snakes. He jests with Cleopatra on the word 'worm' and explains the painless way in which snake poison operates. Cleopatra puts on her robe and regal costume, and is kissed by Iras, who suddenly dies. Cleopatra too takes the poison and dies as a guard rushes in. Charmian also dies. Dolabella enters to discover what has happened and is followed by Caesar, who has suspected that something drastic may take place. After examining the bodies Dolabella finds a bleeding wound on Cleopatra's arm and a guard finds 'an aspic's trail'. Caesar promises an honourable burial for Cleopatra and Antony in the same grave, orders his army to be at the funeral, then returns to Rome.

Commentary

Among many areas of interest in this lengthy concluding scene, four emerge as particularly noteworthy.

Cleopatra disguises her intentions from Caesar. He attempts to hide from her his intention to lead her in triumph through Rome. Cleopatra wins their final battle of mutual deception; she outwits Caesar (with assistance from Dolabella) and sees behind his charming exterior. The direct confrontation between them is something of an anti-climax and it is not inappropriate that their leading topic of conversation should centre upon finances – the symbol of power and authority. Theirs has been a political battle. Cleopatra chooses to die rather than to submit to Caesar's authority, so with her death she triumphs over him. Her will has defied his wishes.

Cleopatra's memories of Antony contain images of sleep, dreams, nature, sexual fecundity – 'His delights/Were dolphin-like' – and the sun and the moon. Antony's love irradiated their universe and ennobled it:

His face was as the heavens, and therein stuck
A sun and moon, which kept their course, and lighted
The little O, the earth.

Notice that Cleopatra uses hyperbole to describe Antony: their conflicts are forgotten. Her memories, and poetic descriptions, serve to show that the imagination has triumphed over political realities. She does not attempt to ingratiate herself with Caesar, preferring imaginative over-romanticized memories of her time with Antony. In other words reality has taken second place to dreams.

The clown with his basket is not an uncommon figure in Shakespearian tragedy. Parallels are found in the graveyard scene of *Hamlet* and the Porter episode in *Macbeth*. The clown prose episode acts (a) as comic relief, a psychological release of tension (b) as a commentary on what is to take place – there are puns and jests on death and dying – notice that the worm is a symbol of mortality (c) as a commentary on the themes of the play: appearance and reality; the brevity of human existence; equality in death if not in life.

Caesar's reaction to Cleopatra's death is revealing. He has to find how it took place, how he was deceived. Caesar is methodical to the last. Generously he allows joint burial and in his prosaic way pays tribute to Cleopatra's bravery and fame. Earlier he allows Cleopatra to retain her fortune (although here double motives may be operating – he has an ulterior motive, which is to win her confidence). He accords proper dignified funeral rites to Antony and Cleopatra. However 'their story' is eclipsed by 'his glory which/Brought them to be lamented'. Caesar is full of self-importance and the play closes with him, the sole authority, giving orders.

better i.e. a more certain, a nobler.

Not being . . . will Caesar is not Fortune, merely a slave of fortune.

shackles accidents Prevents things happening.

bolts up change Stops changes in fortune.

Which sleeps . . . Caesar's Notice that Cleopatra is saying she need never again taste the earth which is dungy and the fruits of which nourish both the beggar and Caesar. Remember that 'dung' also occurred in the very first scene of the play; it now appears towards the end almost as a bridging word, or a *motif* conveying meaning – all is dung, clay and vanity.

as Will make me.

full reference Fully refer yourself. Note the alliterative 'f' and 'e' sounds to convey a sense of freedom, and the repetition of 'full' in the next line in order to emphasize his master's benevolence.

doctrine Lesson.

You see . . . surpris'd It seems that whilst Proculeius and Cleopatra have been talking, Gallus and his soldiers have crept up into the monument in order to capture her. (This speech is attributed in modern editions to Gallus).

Reliev'd Rescued; a continuation of the 'beggar' metaphor – beggars were relieved by charity.

of death too . . . our dogs of languish i.e. relieved of death. The meaning is that even dogs are not allowed to waste away and to die. 'Languish' refers to a wasting disease.

Let the world . . . come forth The world has to see how noble Caesar is; if you die his nobility will not show itself.

Worth many . . . beggars (a) death commonly takes babes and beggars; (b) I (Cleopatra) am worth more than babes and beggars; (c) an echo of the previous beggar references.

mortal house i.e. her body.

water-flies . . . abhorring An image of water-flies covering her with eggs until she looks abhorrent. Cf. her words to Antony, III, 13: 'Lie graveless, till the flies and gnats of Nile/Have buried them for prey!'

trick Habit, custom.

If it might please ye/This face Dolabella's words are lost in Cleopatra's fantasy.

His legs bestrid the ocean Perhaps in her dream Antony resembles the statue that was reputed to have been over the entrance to Rhodes harbour in the Aegean Sea.

his rear'd arm/Crested the world An image from heraldry – a 'rear'd arm' on a helmet or coat of arms.

His voice . . . spheres His voice had the properties of the harmony of the spheres. The earth was supposed to be at the centre of nine moving spheres, each of which made a note of music; the movement of the nine together was the 'music of the spheres' which human beings couldn't hear.

to friends i.e. during everyday conversation.

grew the more by reaping An image from gathering in the harvest: i.e. the more Antony's bounty was accepted the more it was practised and dispensed (as with gathering the harvest in the Autumn, the more there is, the more to be reaped).

dolphin-like The dolphin was regarded as the king of the sea-kingdom; playful, happy – dolphins were famous for their antics.

in his livery . . . crownets Kings were in Antony's service. A list of monarchs said to be controlled by him is found in III,6.

plates Silver coins.

Nature wants stuff . . . fancy Nature lacks the material to compete with the imagination.

shadows i.e. the figment of the imagination. Cleopatra is saying that although nature cannot compete with the imagination Antony was far greater than anything the imagination can conceive.

As answering to the weight i.e. in a manner corresponding to the heavy loss.

Would I might never . . . success May I never succeed in my objectives.

Which is the Queen of Egypt? (a) Cleopatra may be curtseying before Caesar and hence cannot be distinguished from her servants (b) in her 'desolation' Cleopatra is dressed in the manner of her servants (c) Caesar may be sarcastic – 'is there an Egyptian Queen any longer?'

we will extenuate rather than enforce i.e. we will be considerate rather than harsh.

lay on me a cruelty Make it seem that I am cruel.

Your scutcheons Shields – trappings of conquest and power.

brief List.

What . . . back? Cleopatra seems to move threateningly towards Seleucus.

estates Positions.

To one so meek Irony: she hasn't acted meekly towards Seleucus: why she thinks Caesar may be taken in by this is a mystery. Probably an illustration of Cleopatra's increasing loss of practical acumen – her thoughts are elsewhere.

parcel Add one more to.

Immoment toys Insignificant toys, of no consequence.

modern Ordinary.

Livia Caesar's wife.

cinders . . . chance Another image from fire and ashes: what remains alive and burning in my spirit in spite of my destroyed fortunes ('the ashes of my chance').

Forbear Leave.

We answer . . . name We have to answer for the errors made by others in our name.

make prize with you Haggle with you about the price of.

sold i.e. to you in the first place.

we intend so to . . . counsel We intend to make arrangements for you as you yourself shall advise.

I should not . . . myself i.e. commit suicide.

Whispers Charmian This stage direction (witnessed by the audience) increases the dramatic suspense – what does she say?

Finish, good lady Notice that Iras does not like secrets to be kept from her.

Hie Hurry.

makes religion to obey Obeys as a religious obligation.

puppet i.e. metaphorically.

rules Rulers.

lictors Roman officials who like the Parish beadles of Shakespeare's day whipped criminals and prostitutes.

catch at Lay hands on.

scald Mean, distasteful.

Ballad us . . . tune Make ballads up about us and sing them out of tune.

Extemporally i.e. in an unrehearsed exaggerated manner.

forth i.e. on the stage.

boy my greatness An ironic comment – Cleopatra, on the Shakespearian stage, would have been performed by a boy. Notice that Cleopatra's metaphors from the stage and acting a part serve to reinforce the harsh reality of the situation. Cleopatra has performed before Caesar; he has tried also to play games with her. She now realizes that her performance is over, and so is her life which amounted to so much more than simply a boy actor imitating the behaviour of a whore.

my nails . . . eyes i.e. she will pluck her eyes out with her nails.

I am again . . . Cydnus i.e. I will dress as I did then.

chare Task.

marble-constant As firm and fixed as marble.

now the . . . of mine The changing moon is a symbol of change, and of the goddess Isis represented by Cleopatra.

Clown i.e. a simple man.

lie A pun; to tell an untruth; lie down as if dead; to copulate.

falliable Certain.

worm will do his kind Act according to nature.

dress her not i.e. to be cooked in hell.

whoreson Foul.

Give me . . . crown Before she dies she puts on the dress of the authority which has been taken from her.

Immortal longings Longings to be immortal. The repetitive alliterative 'm' and 'n' sounds add to the effect of desire for eternity, as do the 'n' and 'o' sounds of the monosyllabic 'Now no more'.

yare, yare Quickly, quickly.

their after wrath Their giving them bad luck: 'their' refers to the 'gods' not to 'men'.

that name i.e. of Antony's wife.

title Claim.

other elements i.e. earth and water.

aspic The asp (a viper, or poisonous snake).

This i.e. Iras's death.

make demand of her Inquire about Cleopatra.

spend . . . to have (a) he'll waste a kiss on Iras (b) he'll kiss her instead of saving it for me: the kiss will be to me as heaven.

mortal wretch Deadly creature. Cleopatra puns at her own expense – she'll soon be no longer 'mortal'.

intrinsicate Intricate; intimate; basic; inmost.

Unpolicied i.e. his plans have all come to nothing.

eastern star Cleopatra; the morning star.

break (a) the self (b) the heart.

Nay I . . . too Probably addressed to Charmian: she too must kill herself.

Applying . . . arm Curious stage direction, as the Clown appears to have brought in one asp only.

Downy windows Soft eyelids.

Phoebus The sun.

crown's awry . . . it Loyal to the end she straightens her mistress's crown so that she can die in her complete and ordered nobility.

play i.e. my part. The theatrical metaphor is continued.

feel thee i.e. death.

beguil'd Deceived.

Is this well done? Irony (a) is this proper? (b) has it been done well?

levell'd at Guessed. The metaphor is from taking aim with a weapon.

trimming up Straightening.

strong toil of grace The strength of her charm.

vent of blood A bleeding wound.

blown Swollen.

pursued conclusions infinite Pursued many experiments.

Strike those . . . them Strike with sorrow those who have caused them.

their story is . . . lamented Their tale evokes as much pity as the glory of the man (i.e.Caesar) who is responsible for these lamentable events. Notice that even here Caesar praises himself. His words unfavourably contrast with the unselfish praise Antony gives Brutus at the end of *Julius Caesar*.

Revision questions on Act V

1 Write an account of the ways in which Cleopatra and Caesar attempt to manipulate each other in Act V.

2 What part does the dead Antony play in this Act?

3 Compare and contrast the death of Antony and the death of Cleopatra. Which do you find the more dramatically effective and why?

4 What does the Act reveal about Caesar's character?

5 Consider the role in this Act of (a) Proculeius, (b) Dolabella, (c) the clown, (d) Iras and Charmian.

Shakespeare's art in *Antony and Cleopatra*

Setting

The historical time is 30 BC, Rome is the dominant power, the centre of an Empire stretching into Asia. It is controlled by a feuding triumvirate, the generals Octavius Caesar, Marcus Antonius and Lepidus, who took over after the death of Brutus, Julius Caesar's chief killer. The locations of the play represent the several parts of the Roman Empire and the areas within its sphere of influence: Egypt (Alexandria, Cleopatra's palace); Rome (Caesar's house); Messina, where Sextus Pompeius, who is challenging the triumvirs for power, holds power; Misenum, where the confrontation between the Romans is enacted; Pompey's galley; Syria – a far-flung outpost of the Empire; Actium; the surroundings of Alexandra and the environs of Cleopatra's palace; and Cleopatra's monument near the palace. So the settings range from palaces, the house of Caesar at the heart of the Imperial capital, to outlying border posts, battlefields, ships, and Egyptian monuments. The principal location is Egypt; it is in Egypt that the Romans intrude, bringing their foreign attitudes, conventions, customs and desires.

The Nile is mentioned, as is the Egyptian Goddess Isis and the Roman mythological hierarchy. There seems to have been no scenery or specific period costumes in Shakespeare's theatre; however, in the final scene Cleopatra asks Charmian to 'cut her lace' so that she can breathe. In the opening scene there is the stage direction 'Enter Antony, Cleopatra, her Ladies, the Train, with Eunuchs fanning her', which helps to convey the exoticism of the Egyptian setting. References to cock-fighting, gambling, coursing, hunting, falconry, cards, dice and billiards, point to an Elizabethan rather than a classical setting. Cleopatra uses 'posts' and messengers. Banquets, toasts, much drinking, and a reference to the belief that washing in blood leads to rejuvenation, all indicate the concerns of Shakespeare's contemporaries. Boy actors are mentioned in the line 'some squeaking Cleopatra boy my greatness' (V,2). Antony's 'A haltered neck which does the hangman thank/For being yare about him' (III,11) contains an allusion to the Elizabethan habit of executing gentlemen by using the sword rather than hanging them by the halter reserved for the lower classes.

The setting, the historical time of the play, its social circumstances, and physical location, provide the wellspring for the central antithesis of the drama: the confrontation between Egypt, the representative of the values of love and hedonism, and Rome, the representative of public duty rather than private passion. Antony is a triumvir with administrative responsibilities; his setting is Rome and its empire, the soldiers, the servants of the empire. His has been a background of internal intrigue and civil war, of power struggles, and external threat. The foundation of Roman Imperial power – its Empire – must be maintained.

Cleopatra too is a ruler and a Queen. She is surrounded by those who obey her every command and whim. No internal opposition to her is indicated. She has time to concentrate on personal passion set in her own surroundings, and on passion having political implications. Antony, the object of her desires, is the representative of the potential conquerors of her kingdom – Rome. Cleopatra's language reflects her sensuality, her desires, her longings and her native land. Hers is a world of passions, storms, graves, flies, gnats and the Nile.

Themes

Enumeration of some of the ideas and preoccupations exhibited in *Antony and Cleopatra* illustrates just how diverse, varied and manifold are its themes: the tragic themes; the theme of the limitations of the physical world; of the imagination, of desires; of inner struggle; of experience; of Egypt and Rome; of the value of striving for power and material success; of sexuality; of hedonism and stoicism; of the illusion that action brings results; of political conflict for the control of an Empire; of value, of what price the world, what price love?; of duty against pleasure; of what is love?; of conflict; of age versus youth; of honour and decorum; of extremes and a middle way; of entrapment; of loyalty and desertion; of the power of a woman over a man; of the loss of self-control; of truth versus lying; of the past and the present; of performance, of theatricality; of death and attitudes to it; of self-betrayal; of bungling.

Many of these twenty-eight themes are closely inter-related, and conveyed through opposition, through antithesis of character, setting, situation, images, actions. They are enacted on the personal and private level, the microcosmic level and on the general macrocosmic level. For instance, the age and youth theme transverses the conflict between two generals, Antony and Octavius, for supreme mastery of an Empire, and is associated with the past and with personal characteristics. Antony's generalship, his greatness as a military commander is past, a memory to be recalled, as is shown in the opening lines of the play. Antony is in the line of descent from Hercules, to Julius Caesar, to Pompey the Great. With his death dies the heroic past; the stage, the Empire, is left to the uninspired, dull younger Octavius: 'there is nothing left remarkable/Beneath the visiting moon'. Antony, ironically, represents romantic hope, usually associated with youth and inexperience. With his death 'young boys and girls/Are level now with me' (IV,15). It is the 'scarce-bearded Caesar' (I,1), 'the boy Caesar' (III,13), who opposes the love of Antony 'the old ruffian' (IV,1) for 'a princess/Descended of so many royal kings' (V,2), whom 'age cannot wither' (II,2), and who is 'wrinkled deep in time' (I,5). Octavius spends his youthful years on the business of state. Love is related to the stupidity of old age. Antony's 'white' hairs 'reprove the brown for rashness' (III,11). Caesar personally objects to being called 'boy' by Antony (IV,1). Theirs is a personal conflict as well as a power conflict and a fight for political dominance.

Antony and Cleopatra is a tragedy, a personal tragedy that differs slightly in degree of emphasis from classical tragedy, in which a noble person of high birth struggles against the inevitable. It is true that Antony's good luck, his protecting gods have deserted him, but his tragedy and Cleopatra's is of their own making. They sacrifice power, duty, responsibility for love and desire. Antony is entrapped within a grand infatuation from which he cannot free himself. Cleopatra too is entombed with memories of Antony. Part of the tragedy is the witnessing of a once great man defeated in a struggle for power by a younger, more calculating man. On the other hand, part of the tragedy lies in the display of self-destruction and personal humiliation by a man of honour and nobility. Caesar's messenger Thidias is whipped in order to satisfy Antony's personal frustration and sense of power over inferiors. A brave general deserts in the middle of a battle in order to follow a woman. A great general is unable to kill himself properly, and loses self-control. Dominated by a woman, he commits suicide as the consequence of a lie, a game of Cleopatra's. It has frequently been pointed out that *Antony and Cleopatra* has much in common with the Shakespearian tragedy immediately preceding it, *Macbeth*. In both a great commander is unduly under feminine influence and is consequently destroyed. Both tragic heroes turn on their women: 'this foul Egyptian hath betrayed me' (IV,11). Both achieve some liberation in death.

An obvious theme of the play is the power of sexual passion over duty and responsibility – a theme expounded in the opening lines of the play: 'The triple pillar of the world' Antony has, according to Philo, become 'transform'd/Into a strumpet's fool.' The play explores through imagery, antithesis, settings and contrasts, the nature of the relationship between Antony and Cleopatra enacted against the background of the mystery and creative fecundity of Egypt and the Nile. At the conclusion of the tragedy mutual suicide, the deliberate throwing off of the physical aspect of existence, brings the lovers together, reconciles them and shows the victory of imagination and poetry over reason and the material.

Antony and Cleopatra enter death as lovers: Antony says 'I will be/A bridegroom in my death, and run into't/As to a lover's bed' (IV,14). In the final act Cleopatra imagines being with Antony in eternity. As she dies she thinks she hears 'Antony call'. He mocks 'The luck of Caesar', their spirits are together; 'my other elements/I give to baser life'. Her choice of suicide rather than submission shows the triumph of love and desire over physical reality. Love has ultimately triumphed.

The characters

Antony

'you shall see in him/ The triple pillar of the world transform'd/Into a strumpet's fool.'

The opening speech of *Antony and Cleopatra* pinpoints succinctly what has happened to Antony. A brave respected General 'is become the bellows and the fan/To cool a gipsy's lust'. Shakespeare in this play does not show us the young Antony (for him we must look at *Julius Caesar*) but a 'Lord of lords' (IV,8), a 'huge spirit' whose decline is now in progress. Antony 'fishes, drinks, and wastes/The lamps of night in revel'. Throughout Antony is described as larger than life in terms of physical prowess, military skills, character, passions, and energy. He is a 'Herculean Roman', an epithet not without its ironic element. Antony is called 'noble' at least eight times but is rarely viewed as such. As the play develops Antony becomes less and less in command of himself, his actions, his personal fate and the countries he controls. Personal and public disintegration join forces. He is rational when discussing Caesar's complaints that Antony denied him 'arms and aid when I required them' (II,2), but displays extreme violent anger with Thidias (III,13), and Cleopatra (IV,12). Cleopatra's kissing of Thidias' hand provides the flash point that provokes Antony's anger, and is a result of suspicion, fear of being replaced in Cleopatra's affections, and rash judgement. His attack on Cleopatra emphasizes physical decay; 'half-blasted' and images of left-over food. Antony, aware of his own weakening, attacks himself; his violence is the product of frustration at the decline of his powers.

Antony, whose 'face was as the heavens' (V,2), and whose death is likened to the end of the universe, in which 'there is nothing left remarkable/Beneath the visiting moon' (IV,15), is described favourably by his enemies. Caesar admits that in Antony 'You shall find there/A man who is the abstract of all the faults/That all men follow' (I,4). He recalls Antony's bravery and courage in defeat (I,4), and admits that 'The death of Antony/Is not a single doom, in the name lay/A moiety of the world' (V,1) which is not merely a tribute to Antony's administrative authority but to his strength. Amongst those close to him he inspires deep affection. The usually cynical Enobarbus calls himself 'an ass, am onion-eyed' (IV,2) when he says farewell, and dies of a broken heart; Eros kills himself rather than Antony. So what has happened to the 'greatest soldier of the world' (I,3)?

Antony resents young Caesar's inexperience (III,13) – he is twenty years older than Caesar – and childishly and unrealistically challenges Caesar to single combat. The future is with Caesar: the soothsayer warns Antony that near Caesar 'thy angel/Becomes afeard; as being o'erpower'd' (II,3). Caesar is endowed with 'natural luck' (II,3), and Antony's luck has run out. In the past, as Antony admits, 'mine hours were nice and lucky' (III, 13); however, 'my good stars, that were my former guides,/Have empty left their orbs, and shot their fires/Into the abysm of hell' (III,13). Hercules, Antony's guardian angel, has left him: as the second soldier indicates prior to the decisive battle, ''Tis the god Hercules, whom Antony lov'd,/Now leaves him' (IV,3), and 'Fortune and Antony part' (IV,12).

Towards the end of the play Antony regains some of his former virtues. He is magnanimous to Enobarbus; indeed, it is Antony's generosity that breaks Enobarbus's spirit. Antony does 'now not basely die' but courageously: 'a Roman, by a Roman/Valiantly vanquish'd' (IV, 15). But throughout the play he is suffering from a disease, his passion for Cleopatra, which obsesses his mind and which causes him to desert his public responsibilities, leave Rome for Alexandria, fly from the battle to pursue Cleopatra. Duty is forsaken, and in Rome Antony confesses 'I' the east my pleasure lies' (II,3). Caesar's final order that Cleopatra 'shall be buried by her Antony./No grave upon the earth shall clip in it/A pair so famous' (V,2), is a recognition of the inevitable, and of their mutual love. Without Cleopatra Antony's life force has gone entirely; 'Since Cleopatra died,/I have liv'd in such dishonour that the gods/Detest my baseness' (IV,14).

Antony is a paradox. He has sacrificed his power, authority, home, duty and friendship for an all-consuming infatuation. Despite this, his friends remain in the truest sense his followers: Enobarbus is heart-broken, Cleopatra is obsessed with memories of him, and kills herself in order to join Antony – 'Methinks I hear/Antony call' (V,2), she says, and 'Husband, I come' (V,2). Perhaps the best summary of his qualities is that provided by the soldier Maecenas: 'His taints and honours/Wag'd equal with him' (V,1).

Much has been written about Antony. For A. C. Bradley, 'He is neither a mere soldier nor a mere sensualist. He has imagination, the temper of an artist who revels in abundant and rejoicing appetites', who 'feasts his senses on the glow and richness of life, flings himself onto its mirth and revelry and yet feels the poetry in all this'. Hazlitt, on the other hand, sees 'irregular grandeur' in his soul, and in the play Antony's moodiness, his self-indulgence, his irresponsibility, his depressions exhibit themselves until his final ecstatic union in death with Cleopatra. His being is determinedly hers. Yet all is not clear, and there are actions of his that are difficult to explain, or actions pointing to serious deficiencies in his character. For instance, it can be argued that his words to Octavia are sincere and that he intends to be faithful to her. Antony may well be taken in by his own words. His action in marrying her is an adoption of the easiest line of political expediency. Or perhaps he deliberately marries her with no intention of being loyal to her.

Again, the reasons for Antony's return to the East are not simply boredom with Octavia, infatuation with Cleopatra and incapability of living without her. His spirit in Rome is dominated by the superior Octavius. He needs to leave Rome to escape his younger rival's influence. In fact, in II,3, it is only after a discussion with the Soothsayer about his luck and his relationship with Octavius that Antony confesses his pleasure lies in the East. There is the suggestion that he needs Cleopatra and Egypt, that his luck has run out in Rome, which he leaves for political reasons and out of considerations of honour.

Much is learned about Antony from other characters, from for instance Philo, Decretas, the Soothsayer, Octavius, Enobarbus, and Scarus, among others. In the final Act Antony is immortalized in Cleopatra's poetry. We learn early on in the play that he is a creature of sexual excess, of loss of control and reason, who is not what he was: as Philo says 'he is not Antony' (I,1). Octavius's first words in the play condemn Antony's loss of masculinity, his excess (I,4), and Scarus observes that after Actium 'Experience, manhood, honour, ne'er before/Did violate so itself' (III,10). Antony has self-awareness, reflecting, when hearing of his wife's death, that 'the present pleasure/By revolution lowering, does become/The opposite of itself' (I,2), and after Actium he tells his supporters to go to Caesar because he has 'fled myself' – that is, lost his reason (III,11).

Antony has overflowed his measure whereas Octavius has remained full and controlled. The metaphor from a measuring cup is an appropriate one. Antony has lost his self to Cleopatra.

Octavius fills the vacuum left in Imperial power, control and authority, by Antony's loss of self. The Roman aspect of Antony asserts itself when he rounds on Cleopatra, telling her 'Though you can guess what temperance should be/You know not what it is' (III,13). Octavius says that Antony wastes time through revelling (I,4). None of the other commentators on Antony's activities deny this. Antony is generous and is compared with Jove; Octavius is mean and controlled. Antony has deliberately chosen to lose himself. Octavius fights for supremacy of an Empire, of control and self-assertion. Appropriately Antony's friends desert him and go over to Octavius, for Antony's desire is to submerge his identity in that of Cleopatra.

Ironically, in the play the display of the ancient Roman virtues associated with the mythological figures of Mars and Hercules comes not from Octavius but from accounts of how Antony used to be, given by Octavius. He recalls in I,4 Antony's former heroism, bravery, endurance; his warrior qualities. Antony accepts his rival's challenge to fight a naval battle, not from strategic considerations. He ignores the opposition of his loyal companions to the idea: honour probably demands that he fight Octavius at sea, and Cleopatra wishes it. Antony's motives are, as has been remarked, often unclear and at times complex. Decisions are affected, as he recognizes, by his moods. He tells his attendants after Actium to 'take the hint/Which my despair proclaims' (III,11).

In IV,2 Antony takes farewell of his servants, thus anticipating an unfavourable outcome to the following day's battles. The scene displays his absolute honesty, interpreted by Enobarbus as mental aberration: "Tis one of those odd tricks which sorrow shoots/Out of the mind.' Influenced by Enobarbus's objections, he then attempts to perform, to erect a façade of optimism and to 'drown consideration' (IV,2). Thus he is easily influenced, but only too self-aware. Antony's weaknesses are admirably summed up by Pompey in II,1. He is a 'libertine' who is tied up, entrapped 'in a field of feasts' which 'keep his brain fuming'. Antony's 'honour' and self are being consumed; his sexual desires have led him into becoming a servant to Cleopatra. The first lines of the play indicate his effeminacy and lack of masculinity. Cleopatra even puts on his clothing, and in a most un-Roman manner wears 'his sword Philippan' (II,5). Octavius comments that 'the queen of Ptolemy' is not 'more womanly than he' (I,4). Antony believes that Cleopatra has emasculated him, saying to Mardian 'O, thy vile lady!/She has robb'd me of my sword' (IV, 14). Enobarbus appropriately sums up what has happened to Antony; he 'only, that would make his will/Lord of his reason' (III,13).

At the end of the drama Cleopatra, obsessed with the dead Antony, sees him as a superhuman whose 'legs bestrid the ocean' (V,2). His physical body after his death is 'this case of that huge spirit' (IV,15). Throughout Antony has desired to escape himself, his background, responsibilities, time. He escapes himself through entrapment to Cleopatra. His death represents his own and then Cleopatra's final material liberation: at the conclusion of the drama Antony's spirit has soared triumphant.

Cleopatra

Age cannot wither her, nor custom stale
Her infinite variety: other women cloy
The appetites they feed, but she makes hungry,
Where most she satisfies

Cleopatra is a paradox. Her creation and conception are not without their problems. On Shakespeare's stage Cleopatra, a mature, attractive, sensual, complex woman, is performed by a boy. A reason she gives in the final scene of the play for not wishing to be led in triumph by Caesar through Rome is that 'I shall see/Some squeaking Cleopatra boy my greatness/I' the posture of a whore'. At the beginning she cannot endure 'A Roman thought' (I,2); at the end she dies 'after the high Roman fashion' (IV,15). Her love for Antony is possessive, yet she too depends on it. When he is dead her thoughts dwell on their past together, and her final words echo with 'O Antony!' We witness her experiencing diverse changes of mood, yet at the culmination of the drama she has 'nothing/Of woman in me: now from head to foot/I am marble-constant' (V,2). Variety, inconstancy, as she admits, are part of her femininity.

Cleopatra is compared with 'the goddess Isis' (III,6) whose costume she wears, is 'cunning past man's thought' (I,2): frequently, especially with Antony and Caesar, she is shown in situations where manipulative cunning is required. She manages to trick Caesar in the end and is able to kill herself. Cleopatra is an 'enchanting queen' (I,2), a 'great Fairy' (IV,8), a 'witch' (IV,12). She is described as 'a strumpet', as a 'wrangling Queen! /Whom everything becomes' and in whom 'every passion fully strives/To make itself, in thee, fair and admired!' (I,1). She is an 'Egyptian dish', and a 'whore' (I,1; III,6). Antony is by no means her first lover. Images of fertility remain with her, as do those of sensuality. In her 'witchcraft join with beauty, lust with both' (II,1). Other characters tell us that she loves to 'wander through the streets' (I,2), Enobarbus claims that he 'saw her once/Hop forty paces through the public street' (II,2). When first she became Julius Caesar's lover she was brought to him rolled up in a mattress (II,6).

She appears in sixteen of the forty scenes. She dominates Acts I and V. Even when absent from stage, her presence is felt. From the opening speech of the play we learn of her 'tawny front', entrapment of a great general, and 'gipsy's lust'. Her entrance is a grand one, accompanied by Antony, 'her Ladies, the train, with Eunuchs fanning her'. Her authority and command are emphasized. She dominates Antony in the opening exchanges, although her first line 'If it be love indeed, tell me how much' points to the forever searching, questing, explorative nature of her personality. She teases, wrangles and resists the definite, whilst playing on Antony's weak spots, reminding him of his wife and public responsibilities. Much of her power rests in her physical beauty and eroticism, suggested by the impact she has on others, by her imagery and actions and by unspoken body language. In Scene 2 she seems to be searching for Antony; is displeased with him for his 'Roman thought', sends Enobarbus to find him; learns that he is approaching and refuses to see him. She is as ever-changing as the Nile flowing through Egypt. In Scene 3 she is still searching for Antony, and sends a servant to observe him and deliberately to mislead him as a demonstration of her power over him: 'If you find him sad/Say I am dancing'. She is manoeuvring him, playing elaborate games with him, says she is 'sick and sullen', threatens to collapse, rails at him, recalls their past love, denounces his falsity, all in an effort to get him to remain with her and not to return to Rome. She commands the stage, leaving Antony impotently attempting to utter a few words – 'my dearest queen – . . . The gods best know– . . .' Indeed it is not until line 41 that he is able to speak at length. Cleopatra deliberately angers Antony, accusing him 'of excellent dissembling'. However, sensing that she has gone too far and been too egoistic, she reaffirms her love for Antony and his importance in her life: 'my oblivion is a very Antony'. Her very identity and existence revolve around him. Such revelations of utter dependence are rare.

Cleopatra's true self and sense of self are defined through

erotic encounter. She recalls her past sexual adventures with great men; she is no inexperienced girl, but carries 'Phoebus's amorous pinches black/And wrinkled deep in time' – in other words the representative of the eternal ancient amorous energies of sensuality, lust, eroticism, and lasciviousness. She has a dark sensuality, suggesting that she has a dark face or is mysteriously sensual. Her language and thoughts are also violent, representative of her frustration. Yet she loyally and dutifully writes to Antony every day.

Act II Scene 1 contains Pompey's description of her as 'Salt Cleopatra', as lustful with 'waned', pale sensuous 'lip'. It contrasts with Enobarbus's description of her in Scene 2. Pompey draws attention to her mysterious qualities of 'witchcraft' which have entrapped Antony; Enobarbus focuses on her mystical magnificence, comparing her to the goddess Venus. Cleopatra is charismatic; she illuminates everything, and it is no wonder that Antony fell a victim to her spell. Enobarbus's description follows Antony's agreement to marry Octavia, and places Octavia, and Antony's politically motivated expedient, in a wider context. Octavia pales into insignificance beside Cleopatra, who is described as a paradox in nature. It is Cleopatra who animates nature with love, and not nature animating her. The waters follow Cleopatra's barge 'As amorous of their strokes'. It is her barge that burns the water, not the sun burning both. In a sense she has replaced the sun as the source of life. Her sexuality is unending, unsatisfying, for she 'makes hungry/Where most she satisfies'.

Some of the negative sides of her character are displayed in II,5, when the messenger appears with news of Antony's marriage to Octavia. She wants the messenger to tell her what she wants to hear, deliberately bribing him with gold, almost provoking him to lie, then will not listen to him. When she hears that Antony has married Octavia she turns upon the messenger like a hurt, spoilt girl, curses him, and physically assaults him. Aware of her own immense power, she draws a knife on him. Her anger reflects her feeling for Antony, which has caused a total loss of dignity and self-control before social inferiors. Her vanity has been assailed: jealous and inquisitive, she asks for pity and sends out for information on Octavia's physical features. In this scene Cleopatra's moods have oscillated from bawdy merriment, to hopeful expectation, to violent anger and rage, to self-pity, jealousy, and recollection of her power over Antony.

By III,3 when the messenger returns with information on Octavia, Cleopatra has had time to simmer down. Naturally the messenger is afraid of Cleopatra, and in order to flatter her, deliberately gives an unflattering picture of her rival. He is appealing to Cleopatra's highly developed vanity, especially where her physical appearance is concerned. Octavia has qualities Cleopatra places a low estimate on: brown eyes; low forehead; low voice; undignified walk; lack of animation. Cleopatra interrupts his description and turns it to her own advantage in order to satisfy her own ego. She allows herself to be flattered, deceived, and deluded. The messenger's report, a difficult one to give in the first place, and Cleopatra's deliberate distortions of it, draws attention to an important theme in the play and one directly concerning Cleopatra – the theme of truth. We do not know if the messenger's report is true or not, whether it has any accuracy or not. Cleopatra's rearranged report, in which Octavia is 'dull of tongue and dwarfish' is inaccurate. She is playing games with the messenger, with herself and with fidelity. Such games are to lead to Antony's death, and raise the whole issue of viewpoint. Antony continually exaggerates Cleopatra's attractions, Enobarbus's view of her as Venus is hyperbolic. What is the truth about her, or is Cleopatra like the Nile, for ever flowing onward and changing?

III,7 exhibits her wilful stubbornness and the assumption of qualities usually associated with masculinity. She insists on aiding Antony with naval support and her physical presence at the scene of the battle. She brushes aside Enobarbus's wise counsel that her presence will reflect negatively upon Antony's masculine reputation: 'Your presence needs must puzzle Antony . . . He is already/Traduc'd for levity, and 'tis said in Rome/That Photinus, an eunuch, and your maids/Manage this war' – words infuriating Cleopatra into an assertion of her role 'as the president of my kingdom'. She is a monarch with responsibilities, which at times she reveals she has by no means forgotten. The confrontation between her and Antony after Actium is a powerful one. She now has total control over him in personal emotional terms as well as political terms. Cleopatra's influence has resulted in the loss of her personal and political honour. The scene reveals Cleopatra's depth of feeling for him, her acknowledgement of short-sightedness – 'I little thought/You would have followed' – and commitment to the defeated Antony now at the nadir of his fortunes, whom she could so easily have rejected. In fact with the loss of material power, and Antony's increasing dependence upon Cleopatra, their love grows stronger, and they manage to transcend themselves and to merge with each other.

Cleopatra's linking of her fate with Antony's is indicated by her use of the personal pronoun in her question to Enobarbus at the beginning of III,13: 'What shall we do, Enobarbus?' and her loss of confidence contained in her 'Is Antony, or we, in fault for this?' where she uses the royal 'we'. Her contradictory, puzzling mysterious nature emerges in her behaviour towards Thidias in this scene: is she exercising gratuitous power over Octavius's representative, or does she really hope to manipulate him in order to influence Octavius? Is she planning to betray the luckless Antony, enjoying her power over people; is she possibly what Antony thinks she is; a treacherous whore who is going to turn to a more powerful lover? Or is she in this scene playing tricks, this time with Thidias in order to deceive Octavius and remain faithful to Antony? By the end of Act IV Cleopatra is again viewed by Antony in a dual role; she is as much a victim of his moods as he is of hers. On the one hand, when he returns triumphant from battle she is Antony's 'nightingale', and his 'girl' (IV,8), yet by IV,12 she has 'betrayed' him, and is a 'Triple-turn'd whore', whom in defeat he blames and sends from his sight. This rage and turn of mood provokes Cleopatra into what becomes her final, fatal trick. Her test of Antony's love – at the suggestion of Charmian she will 'send him word' of her 'death' (IV,13) – in fact literally leads to her lover's death. The lie, the trick, misfires, and has tragic consequences which she could not have foreseen.

The last scene of Act IV and the final scene of the play (V,2) are dominated by Cleopatra in which, through great poetry, she reveals the extent of her passion for Antony, who has become her 'lord' and without whom she cannot live, being forced to 'come' (IV,15) to him in eternity. In fact her imagination takes hold of her and controls her. Antony is posthumously transformed into a superhuman figure controlling the universe – in a sense he controls her universe. She is theatrical to the last, dying as an Empress, ordering her servants – loyal to her even in death – 'Give me my robe, put on my crown, I have/Immortal longings in me' (V,2). In the manner of her death she is all too human. Charmian observes after she has died that her 'crown's awry,/I'll mend it, and then play'. Appearances have to be maintained even after death.

Cleopatra is human and fallible, but the loyalty she has commanded lives on. In her death she joins Antony and defeats Octavius. Cleopatra's pride will not allow her to be led in triumph through Rome. But even in these scenes mystery surrounds her. The episode with Seleucus, her counsellor, is curious: is she using her treasurer to convince Octavius that she has no wish to die, or does she hope to survive in the world after Antony's death? If she does, then obviously her jewels will be useful: or is she again playing games – perhaps the jewels will pay for her funeral expenses?

Mystery and enigma belong to Cleopatra and are part of her power. It is unclear whether she in fact ordered her ships at Actium to join Caesar's. Such a charismatic character has not been without her defenders. A. C. Bradley has commented on the charge of deliberate betrayal of Antony at Actium: 'Can we feel sure that she would not have sacrificed him if she could have saved herself by doing so? It is not even certain that she did not attempt it. Antony himself believes that she did – that the fleet went over to Octavius by her orders. That she and her people deny the charge proves nothing. The best we can say is that, if it were true, Shakespeare would have made that clear.' She resists formulation and characterization. On stage Cleopatra is dominating, witty, crude, passionate, erotic, jealous, manipulating; but is transformed from a lover teasing Antony into a tragic heroine dying heroically. She is accorded great poetry of memory and imagination, focused not on herself but on Antony. The paradox surrounding her does not disappear. Her mind is no longer fixed on this earth but has leaped into dreams of 'an emperor Antony'. With his death 'there is nothing left remarkable/Beneath the visiting moon' (IV,15). Life is no longer worth living: Antony and Cleopatra are indissolubly united for posterity.

Enobarbus

That truth should be silent I had almost forgot

Hardly noticed in North's Plutarch, Enobarbus is transformed into a major choric character in Shakespeare's play, speaking magnificent poetry and pointed prose. He is the closest of Antony's friends, regrets the hold Cleopatra has over him, yet his great account of her shows that he is by no means unaware of her attractions. Under the pressure of Antony's defeats he deserts him but is forgiven. Full of self-recrimination, he finds a ditch in which to die, 'the foul'st best fits/My latter part of life' (IV,6). His dying words are to ask Antony for forgiveness, the thought that 'the world rank me in register/A master-leaver, and a fugitive', and the repeated 'O Antony! O Antony!' (IV,9).

Domitius Enobarbus is present at many of the most important dramatic confrontations, and his language imaginatively re-creates Cleopatra's sensuous splendour. Described by Antony as 'a soldier only' (II,2), he takes pleasure in his tough, sceptical 'plainness' (II,6). An illustration of his attitudes is seen during his first stage appearance. Alexas comments 'We'll know all our fortunes', to which Enobarbus tartly and aptly replies 'Mine, and most of our fortunes to-night, shall be – drunk to bed' (I,2). He is close to Antony, yet aware of his and others' deficiencies. His choric role as cynical commentator but yet lyrical poet emerges in the lengthy second scene of Act II. During the meeting between the triumvirs his prose quips are silenced by Antony, yet at the end of the scene he is poetically praising Cleopatra in some of the most powerful lines of the play. On board Pompey's galley it is Enobarbus who arranges the drunken triumvirs into a circle and, when they leave the galley, warns them 'Take heed you fall not' (II,7).

Enobarbus has considerable political and personal insight. He is aware that Pompey's days are limited, and tells Lepidus, Antony and Caesar, 'you hear no more words of Pompey' (II,2). He is aware that Octavia is 'of a holy, cold, and still conversation' and that these qualities will result in Antony's return 'to his Egyptian dish again' (II,6). He is only too aware that Antony and Caesar are on a collision course, that 'They'll grind the one the other' (III,5), dares to say that Cleopatra should not interfere in the fighting, telling her correctly that her 'presence needs must puzzle Antony' (III,8). It is he in his choric function who announces the naval defeat: 'To see 't, mine eyes are blasted' (III,10). He is loath to desert Antony, and his words, 'an ass, am onion-eyed' spoken after Antony's farewell to his followers (IV,2), ironically echo his much earlier prosaic quip after hearing of Antony's grief upon Fulvia's (his first wife's) death that 'indeed the tears live in an onion that should water this sorrow' (I,2).

Enobarbus may be regarded as a projection of Antony's other self. His is the cool head and military cunning that Antony lost to Cleopatra. His meanness and cynicism complement Antony's excesses and generosity. It is not without significance that he finally leaves Antony on the night the soldiers hear music taken to represent 'the god Hercules, whom Antony loved' leaving him (IV,3). Antony's generous reaction to Enobarbus's action reflects his positive characteristics. Even in the heat of battle Antony sends on Enobarbus's treasure to him. It is Enobarbus who helps to bring out the best side of Antony; as a soldier remarks to the forlorn Enobarbus: 'Your emperor/Continues still a Jove' (IV,6).

Octavius Caesar

their story is/No less in pity than his glory which/Brought them to be lamented

At the start of the play Octavius is one of the triumvirs, by the end the sole ruler of the Roman Empire. He has liquidated his three political rivals Pompey, Lepidus and Antony. His primary consideration is to obtain power even to the extent of using his own sister Octavia as a pawn in his political ambitions. He gives her to Antony in return for Antony's support in dealing with rebels. Emotionally he remains unaffected by Cleopatra, though there are hints in III,6 that he is upset by what appears to be his sister's humiliation: she comes 'not /Like Caesar's sister', and is 'abused/Beyond the mark of thought'. His egocentricity is apparent from his comments and behaviour. At the end of the play his comments on Antony and Cleopatra focus upon himself and 'his glory which/Brought them to be lamented'. The 'solemn' funeral rites are a tribute to himself as conqueror.

Caesar is in stark contrast to Antony. He is young, calculating, and efficient. His soldiers are respectful towards him, not affectionate. Even Antony admires the speed with which he got to Actium. On Lepidus's galley his distaste is shown by his relative silence; he only turns down Menas's murderous plan to get rid of 'These three world-sharers, these competitors' because it would be found out and he would be associated with it (II,7). Antony, before the decisive battle, orders 'Scant not my cups'; he will 'Be bounteous at our meal' (IV,2). The calculating Caesar, on the other hand, will 'feast the army' knowing they fight better on full stomachs (IV,1). Antony's forces who have gone over to him he places 'in the vant,/That Antony may seem to spend his fury/Upon himself' (IV,6).

Having chosen to make an example of Cleopatra he uses innumerable stratagems in order to get her to Rome, sending her false messages and a party of soldiers to creep up upon her. He cannot anticipate Dolabella's personal loyalty to Cleopatra or anticipate her insight. 'He words me, girls, he words me.' The meeting between Caesar and Cleopatra is that between a young calculating politician and an old seasoned one in a much weaker position. His rhetoric is met by her games with her treasurer Seleucus whom she uses as a ploy to mislead Caesar into thinking that he might be able to bribe her into being led captive to Rome.

Caesar is a practical politician, cold and calculating. His speeches contain few imaginative outbursts, are usually clear and to the point. He does show some generosity to the dead Antony, admitting 'that our stars,/Unreconciliable, should divide/Our equalness to this' (V,1). Even in a funeral oration he is balancing the positives and the negatives.

Octavia

Of a holy, cold, and still conversation

Although Octavia has less than thirty lines in the play she acts as a foil to Cleopatra. Cleopatra has the beauty and Antony's love; Octavia is used as a go-between by her brother and Antony. Enobarbus correctly foresees that she will only provoke Antony's lust for Cleopatra. Octavia is the embodiment of Roman qualities of duty and obedience; she is torn between her husband and her brother, aware of 'no midway 'twixt these extremes at all' (III,4). It is Antony's assumed mistreatment of her which further enrages Caesar against him. A rejected wife, used by her brother as a political pawn, she leaves the play in the middle of Act III. Her brother's Egyptian campaign, Antony and Cleopatra's love are no concern of hers. Octavia is truly 'A more unhappy lady' (III,4) whose disappearance from the action is scarcely noted. Perhaps her one achievement is to have aroused Cleopatra's curiosity and jealousy. Cleopatra sends spies to 'Report the feature of Octavia; her years/Her inclination ... The colour of her hair'. She need not fear.

Octavia's loyalties, affections and duties are divided. In this split state of mind she mutters to herself: 'Husband win, win, brother' (III,4). Further 'Her tongue will not obey her heart, nor can/Her heart inform her tongue' (III,2).

Charmian and Iras

Your fortunes are alike

Charmian is close to her mistress Cleopatra, to whom she gives advice even on love affairs, and it is Charmian who suggests that Cleopatra mislead Antony into thinking that she is dead. Cleopatra tells Charmian the secret of the asp and the fig basket. It is Charmian who cools Cleopatra's temper after she has drawn a knife on the messenger who brings the news of Antony's marriage (II,5), but she can go so far and no further in teasing Cleopatra (I,5). Charmian knows Cleopatra's moods, flatters her and placates her (III,3). To Charmian Cleopatra confides that she 'might sleep out this great gap of time/My Antony is away', to which Charmian replies, 'You think of him too much' (I,5).

Charmian's devotion and loyalty are tested in death. She closes Cleopatra's eyes, puts her crown straight, her words 'Your crown's awry,/I'll mend it and then play' echo Cleopatra's previous words to her, fulfil her duty and ironically comment upon her fate. Her 'play' is to join Cleopatra in death (V,2). She has proved the truth of the Soothsayer's words in the second scene of the play that Charmian 'shall outlive the lady whom you serve'.

Iras usually accompanies Charmian on stage. Her longest speech is in prose in the second scene, echoing Charmian's words about Isis, cuckolding and fortune. It is Iras who prepares Cleopatra for death and who courageously initially takes the poison. Iras cannot see Cleopatra humiliated: 'I'll never see 't! for I am sure my nails/Are stronger than mine eyes' (V,2).

In the second scene the Soothsayer maintains formal verse amid the prose banter of Charmian, Iras and Alexas, whose lively talk and suggestive remarks deflate his seeming profundities. Charmian's first words in the play contain an elaborate sexual joke relating to lust, husbands and cuckoldry. Indeed sexual allusions and licentiousness are never far from what she says and point up the hedonistic elements of the play with its emphasis upon pleasure. Her opening words are a pun on the meaning of the word 'know' (to gain knowledge, and to have sexual experience). At times Charmian has a choric function. For example she tells the Soothsayer that she wishes to 'be married to three kings in a forenoon, and widow them all', thus drawing attention to the motif of insatiable appetites running through the play. Hyperbolic extravagance and fantastic imaginings are by no means confined to Antony and Cleopatra. Charmian desires 'a child at fifty, to whom Herod of Jewry may do homage'. She asks the Soothsayer to 'find one to marry me with Octavius Caesar, and companion me with my mistress'. Her allusions suggestively relate Egypt with the birth of Jesus (i.e. the three kings; thirty years after the events of the play Jesus was born); King Herod; lines in Matthew II,15: 'Out of Egypt have I called my son'; and prefigure the ending of the play, for it is Octavius Caesar who is to triumph. In this way Charmian's suggestive wit not merely places the action in a historical perspective but usurps the Soothsayer's function.

Iras's banter too is not to be ignored: its wit, fun, suggestive lustful innuendoes, also mirror Cleopatra's desires and reflect the atmosphere of the court. Iras's lines are full of ironic phallic suggestiveness. Alexas notes 'We'll know all our fortunes', to which Enobarbus replies that 'most of our fortunes to-night, shall be drunk to bed'. Iras's rejoinder 'There's a palm presages chastity, if nothing else', is word-play on (1) the palm of the hand used for telling fortunes, (2) the noted healing qualities of the palm tree, (3) its associations with virtue.

So in short, Charmian and Iras are part of the fun-loving, hedonistic, bawdy, suggestive element of the play. They mirror their mistress; her lusts, desires, extravagant imaginings, theatricality, and sheer love of life. Their fate reflects Cleopatra's tragedy.

Structure and style

Structure

The commentary to the first scene indicates that within it are the central themes of the drama: 'the triple pillar of the world transform'd/Into a strumpet's fool'; passion versus duty; the neglect of public duty for private passions; the conflict between Antony and Cleopatra, and the differing values of Rome and Egypt; the attempt to hold together a disintegrating Empire. The shifting, contrasting settings illuminate these themes. Accepting the non-Shakespearian five act division, it can be seen that a contrasting pattern emerges. The opening three Alexandrian scenes, with large casts, focused upon Cleopatra, on Antony torn between passion and the calls of Rome, give way to the stark setting of Caesar's house in Rome. The play oscillates between these different settings, moving into short, sharp presentations of war viewed from different perspectives until the play's resolution in Cleopatra's monument. The structure reflects the play's themes: Egypt and Rome; Cleopatra and Antony against Caesar; the battle and Antony's defeat; Cleopatra's retreat into her monument; Caesar's victory; truth and illusion; the past and the present; theatricality; love, war and death; death as unity and release; entrapment. The world of Egypt is dominated by Cleopatra, the world of Rome by Caesar. Antony is torn between the two.

The structure of the play has attracted interesting observations. The late Victorian critic, A. C. Bradley in his *Shakespeare's Antony and Cleopatra* (Oxford Lectures on Poetry, 1909), notes the relative lack of action in the opening three acts of the drama. Shifting perspectives, viewing characters from what we as audience are told about their activities, seems to be the activating structural principle. The great 18th-century critic, Dr Johnson, argued that *Antony and Cleopatra*'s episodic structure was one of its virtues: 'the continual hurry of the action, the variety of incidents, and the quick succession of one personage to another, call the mind forward without intermission from the first act to the last. But the power of delighting is derived principally from the frequent changes of the scene.' John Dryden, the late 17th-century dramatist, rewriting *Antony and Cleopatra*, and adapting it for the Restoration stage, believed that there were too many irrelevant scenes in the drama. His play entitled *All for Love, or The World Well Lost* (1677) replaced Eros, Enobarbus, and other characters regarded as minor, by one figure Ventidius, who is upgraded from his Shakespearian role in III,1, set in the far-flung regions of the Roman Empire.

Certain things can be said with some certainty about the structure. Shakespeare didn't divide the play into Acts; these were added in editions published after his death. Yet the action of the play is divided between scenes in Egypt and scenes in Rome. There are domestic scenes and important political ones. Crucial events are described rather than actually presented on stage. Enobarbus describes Cleopatra's arrival; she doesn't literally float down the Nile on her barge: on the Elizabethan stage this would be an impossibility. The sea-battle at Actium occurs off-stage; the audience is told about it. So, telling is crucial to the structure. Cleopatra is not actually seen as Isis; we, the audience, are told about her habit of dressing up as Isis. We do not actually witness Antony's return to Egypt but hear it from Octavius – a far from unbiased source. Structurally, groups of characters from the very opening scene of the play onwards discuss the actions of other characters, usually those of the main protagonists Antony and Cleopatra. These two appear on stage and then leave it; minor characters then appear and discuss what has happened. Another important structural fact: *Antony and Cleopatra* is the second longest of Shakespeare's works and is exceeded in textual length and performing time only by *Hamlet*. It is rarely performed in its entirety on stage.

Analysis of act and scene, enumeration of character appearance, helps to clarify structure. The play has (using the Arden text published by Methuen), forty-two scenes. Antony appears in twenty-two of these, that is, in just over half. Eleven of these appearances are with Cleopatra, five with Caesar. So, in terms of his appearances, the structural balance reflects Antony's preoccupation with Cleopatra rather than with his Roman Imperial responsibilities. Cleopatra appears in sixteen scenes, only five of these being without Antony's actual physical presence, and even in those he dominates her thoughts. So, structurally Antony dominates the relationship. However, more than half of the action of the play is preoccupied not with the private passion of Antony and Cleopatra, but with the power struggle for control of the Empire between Antony and Octavius, and the attempt to keep the Empire intact against internal and external threats.

The opening scenes are representative of structural principles at work in the whole play. Demetrius and Philo, hardly main protagonists, provide differing views on the actions of the main characters. They contrast Rome and Egypt, what Antony may have become, and what he was. After 14 lines Antony and Cleopatra appear and the spotlight switches to them: Cleopatra's first words illustrate themes of the play: 'If', i.e. doubt, uncertainty, differing viewpoints, already introduced by Philo's opening words 'Nay, but'; and the theme of 'love'. The first of the eight messengers, few of whom are well treated, arrives to introduce the world of Rome, politics and responsibility, to be dismissed, and then sought for, by Antony. Thus repetition is a pattern of the structure. Indeed, there is a structural principle of varied repetition represented by: the messengers, their dismissal; desertion and loyalty; innumerable leave takings; returns and departings; handshakes, and the kissing of hands – so easily misunderstood (see Antony's misreading of Thidias's kissing of Cleopatra's hand). To return to the opening scene, the lovers appear, confirm or deconstruct what has been said about them. They leave, and at the end of the scene Philo and Demetrius re-assume their role as observers. The pattern is one of repetition, gossip, observation, and departure.

The first three scenes focus on love. They are set in Cleopatra's Alexandrian palace, and the realities of Rome and Antony's public responsibilities intrude only in terms of the news of his wife's death, and in what we are told his role was. Without a transition the action then moves to Rome and to the seat of Roman Imperial power, Octavius's house, but the focus of attention is still on news of Antony's activities. There are various ways of viewing this structure, which operates on principles of contrast. Act I provides an introduction to the main characters and to Antony's conflict. Act II witnesses Antony's attempt to resolve his conflict by appeasing Caesar and accepting his Roman duties. Act III can be seen as the one in which the structural crisis occurs, for Antony is defeated at Actium – remember the defeat is not witnessed, only related. Act IV sees Antony's effort to salvage victory from defeat, his return to Egypt, defeat in battle, and death. Act V concentrates on Cleopatra and her fantasies. Throughout this organization there emerges a pattern of central action, or the re-telling of it, followed by comments on that action. For instance the activities at Actium (III,10–11) are related rather than shown. Enobarbus and Scarus comment, Canidius comments, and then Antony comments on his own actions after they have taken place. Crucial to the overall structure is observation, suggestion and perhaps untruth. (After all, it is Cleopatra's deliberate lie to Antony, her deliberate tricking him into believing that she is dead, which directly results in his actual death.)

As the play proceeds a change in structural procedure takes place. In Act V the focus narrows from the previous shifting perspectives and episodic nature to concentrate on Cleopatra. There is a startling contrast between the fifteen scenes of the densely populated Act IV and the two scenes of Act V. The last scene of the drama is nearly twice as long as the hitherto longest scene in the play: Scene 13 of Act III – also concentrating on Cleopatra and Antony – has 201 lines. V,2 has 365 lines and is dominated by Cleopatra. The setting is fixed, and she is entrapped at her monument to which even Octavius must go. Cleopatra's thoughts are dominated by Antony, whom she longs to join. Viewed in these terms, the structure of the play is episodic, contrasting, shifting in perspective and illuminating themes. Differing viewpoints and spotlights finally focus upon Cleopatra and her desire to die in order to be reunited with her dead lover. All that Caesar can do at the end is physically to ensure that Cleopatra is united with Antony.

Style
Imagery

Imagery dominates the play. Caroline Spurgeon comments in her classic work *Shakespeare's Imagery* that *Antony and Cleopatra* is pervaded by: 'images of the world, the firmament, the ocean and vastness generally. That is the dominating note in the play, magnificence and grandeur.' She isolates the word 'world' as occurring forty-two times in the play. The idea of space, of the universe, is seen as an astronomical frame of reference to the heavens, the sun, the moon, the stars, night and day, and to nature – to the seasons, the tides, the rain, the air, the clouds. Spurgeon writes that the image of the 'world' is 'continually employed in a way which increases the sense of grandeur, power and space, and which fills the imagination with the conception of beings so great that physical size is annihilated and the whole habitable globe shrinks in comparison with them'. Thus the literal minded Caesar's telling Antony in II,2, 'if I knew/What hoop should hold us staunch from edge to edge/O' the world, I would pursue it', synthesizes the domestic image of the 'hoop' – of a metal band holding a barrel together – with that of keeping together the two rivals fighting for possession of the universe.

A similar emotion is expressed in Octavia's 'amazing picture of the gigantic gaping fissures in the round globe packed tight with the bodies of the dead' (Spurgeon), conveyed in her observation on the feud between her husband and brother: 'Wars 'twixt you twain would be/As if the worlds should cleave, and that slain men/Should solder up the rift' (III,4). Enobarbus has a vision of Antony and Caesar scrapping over the world as if it is 'a pair of chaps, no more', merely food to be devoured (III,5). The fight between Antony and Caesar is for 'the world'. Antony is a 'triple pillar of the world', his 'sword/Quarter'd the world, and o'er green Neptune's back/With ships made cities' – imagery of the sword, destruction, the sea, nature, mythology and human construction coalescing in these lines (IV,14).

Images of the heavens and nature are largely confined to the Egyptian scenes, the images of the world traverse the Egyptian and Roman settings, the exotic and the mundane. Many of Cleopatra's images are from nature, and range from the animate to the inanimate worlds. Persuading Antony that she is not cold towards him, she ranges from 'heaven' to 'hail', to 'poison' to 'stone', to 'womb' to 'storm', to 'flies and gnats of the Nile' (III,13). Her imagery, like that of nature itself, extends from the microcosm, the smallest gnat and fly, to the heavenly macrocosm. Natural images extend from Antony's general 'Then must thou needs find out new heaven new earth', to his more specific 'The April's in her eyes, it is love's spring,/And these the showers to bring it on' (III,2). These images include the Soothsayer's maxim: 'In nature's infinite book of secrecy/A little I can read' (I,2) and encompass Cleopatra's hyperbolic imaginative plea: 'O sun,/Burn the great sphere thou mov'st in, darkling stand/The varying shore o' the world' (IV,15). They are associated with both Antony and Cleopatra. The fecundity of nature, its diversity and richness, serves to explain their relationship. The nature of the imagery serves to pinpoint the contrast between the two worlds and sets of dramatic values in *Antony and Cleopatra*: Rome and Egypt.

Mythological and classical figures, Greek and Roman, Isis, Venus, Jupiter, Apollo, Bacchus, Mercury, Juno, Hercules, Dido, Aeneas and others, are associated with Antony and Cleopatra. When Antony is dead Cleopatra conceives him in terms of 'Jove'. She laments 'Had I great Juno's power,/The strong-wing'd Mercury should fetch thee up,/And set thee by Jove's side' (IV,15). Antony is transformed in her imagination into a gigantic god whose 'legs bestrid the ocean' and whose 'rear'd arm/Crested the world' (V,2). Cleopatra is associated with the moon, she is 'our terrene moon' (III,11), dresses up as Isis 'In the habiliments of the goddess Isis' (III,6) and is linked with the planet Venus (I,5). In classical mythology Venus became the lover of Mars, the Roman god of war. Antony is the representative of Rome. He is a demi-Atlas (I,5), and three times he is seen as the image of Hercules (I,3; II,5; IV,10).

Images of war and conflict surround Rome. Its past is associated with battles. Philo's opening speech of the play remembers Antony as a great soldier, 'those his goodly eyes/That o'er the files and musters of the war/Have glow'd like plated Mars'. Caesar's memory of Antony in his prime piles up images of 'beaten', 'slew'st', 'famine', 'fought'st', 'savages' and 'suffer' (I,4). Octavia pleading with Antony not to fight Caesar, her brother, repeats 'Praying', 'pray', 'prayer', 'Prays' (III,4). Her imagination is as restricted as the martially based environment from which she springs. Her expression does not vary. Antony transcends this world into the Egyptian one of unrestricted imagination, mythology and legend.

This brief image survey should not be concluded without drawing attention to one of the many image patterns in the play. It is perhaps Shakespeare's most sensual and bawdy drama. Clearly images of swords rising and falling, Antony physically rising and falling and disintegrating, have sexual implications. A major theme of the drama is the passion between Antony and Cleopatra and its tragic consequences. The passion is suggested through many kinds of images ranging from allusions to mythological lovers, Nissus, Cupid, Narcissus, to overt references to cuckoldry. Cleopatra's desire in I,5 'to drink mandragora' represents her wish to 'sleep out this great gap of time' whilst her lover is away. It is also an evocation of desire, mandragora being a sleeping-draught made from the mandrake plant which is shaped like the male sexual organs. In the same scene the castrated, 'unseminared', slaves who surround her represent her loss.

Poetry

Stylistically *Antony and Cleopatra* is said to have characteristic features of Shakespeare's later plays, where the ideas are suggestive and densely packed together, and there is a tendency away from excessive use of rhyming couplets. The basic poetic style is blank verse (lines of iambic pentameter usually unrhymed) upon which Shakespeare works infinite variations. Rhyming couplets are rare, mark the conclusion of a few scenes, and emphasize aphorisms. Antony's reflections on the death of his first wife Fulvia in I,2 achieve aphoristic couplet expression: 'she's good, being gone,/The hand could pluck her back that shov'd her on'. In I,3 Charmian's truism 'I wish, forbear;/In time we hate that which we often fear' uses the couplet form, and the song sung by the drunken triumvirs aboard Pompey's galley utilizes this couplet form so common in Shakespeare's earlier dramatic poetry.

Metaphors, similes, mythological allusions, exaggerations, contrasts, violent language, variations in rhythms, extensive use of caesura, and end-stopped and run-on lines are some of the devices giving the poetry of the play its infinite variety. Philo's opening speech provides a useful illustration of some of these techniques at work. It starts in the middle of a thought sequence and gets no further than 'Nay' before there is a caesura; the first three words 'Nay, but this' are monosyllabic and serve to stress the implications of the next word 'dotage', with its threefold sense of infatuation, old age and sleepiness. Three 'o' sounds close togther in 'dotage of our' convey the feeling of shock, surprise and amazement being expressed by Philo. The subject of his attention, 'our general' is introduced at the end of the iambic pentameter line which is not end-stopped but run-on. The poetry conveys the sense: 'Nay, but this dotage of our general's/O'erflows the measure'; and immediately there is the image of excess, the metaphor being taken from a liquid which has overflowed the measuring cup. The opening lines are also full of repetitions, antithesis, alliteration, assonance: 'files and musters', 'glow'd like plated Mars', 'now bend, now turn', 'bend', 'burst', 'buckles', 'breast', 'bellows'.

A feature of the play is the manner in which the characters use blank verse appropriate to their personalities and situations. Enobarbus's great description at the end of the second scene of Act II, discussed in some detail in the commentary to the scene, should be placed in the perspective of other magnificent poetry. Caesar's lines and choice of words are careful and lucid. Alliteration is a feature of his dislikes. Thus in I,4 he compares Antony's Egyptian activities to those who 'Pawn their experience to their present pleasure' – the repetitive alliterative 'p' sounds effectively expressing his distaste. On occasions he expresses himself by the use of appropriate assonance. He tells Lepidus 'Let's grant it is not/Amiss to tumble on the bed of Ptolemy' (I,4) with the assonantal 'to tumble' gaining effect from the reference to Ptolemy, the brother of Cleopatra whom she had married. He can make apt antithesis. Thus in II,7, amidst the drunken revels on Pompey's galley, he scorns Antony's toast with the words, 'It's monstrous labour when I wash my brain/And it grow fouler'. The contrast between washing and growing fouler conveys his contempt for the proceedings. Caesar's rare revelations of personal emotion tend to be displayed in apostrophic invocations addressed to absent persons. In I,4 he calls upon the absent Antony to 'Leave' his 'lascivious wassails' and in doing so uses powerful alliterative assonance. The surprise return of his sister Octavia to Rome without sufficient pomp and ceremony receives Caesar's short, clipped, run-on lines and a chronicle-like recital of kings who have pledged allegiance to Antony, Caesar's rhythmic emphasis stressing the relative comparative power of Antony's allies and Caesar's enemies.

Antony's verse is more varied than Caesar's and often mixes hyperbole, alliteration, and elaborate word play. In his first extensive address to Cleopatra the effect of the cosmic imagery is heightened by the use of caesura, run-on line, monosyllabic form: 'Let Rome in Tiber melt, and the wide arch/Of the rang'd empire fall'. The poetic line seems to collapse with the image of disintegration. Antony's verse is characterized by the mixture of opposites: Rome collapses into its own river; the Roman empire collapses upon itself.

At times the tone of his verse is reflective, meditative, and idiomatic. He justifies his treatment of Caesar's messenger, telling Caesar that 'next day/I told him of myself, which was as much/As to have ask'd him pardon. Let this fellow/Be nothing of our strife' (II,2). Anger takes hypermetric repetitive, staccato form, followed by run-on lines, explanations and rhetorical questions. Thidias activates his anger, and he orders:

Whip him. Were't twenty of the greatest tributaries
That do acknowledge Caesar, should I find them
So saucy with the hand of she here, – what's her name,
Since she was Cleopatra? Whip him, fellows (III,13)

In the first line the repetitive 'w' sounds, the juxtaposition of monosyllables with complex syllabic words such as 'tributaries' that run on across the line to 'acknowledge', the use of the shortened form 'Were't' with the 't' sound emphasized eight times in the line, are all assisted by the length of the lines, which extend beyond the standard iambic pentameter. Similarly, the largely monosyllabic third line is reinforced by a caesura, repetitive 's' sounds, a lengthening out of the line which runs on into the next. The poetic techniques serves to emphasize the changes of mood within Antony, whose anger with Thidias is but an expression of his frustration.

Cleopatra's poetry is a reflection of her changeability, of her 'infinite variety' of temperament and mood. Short sentences of dialogue at the beginning of I,3 – 'Where is he?' 'If you find him sad,/Say I am dancing', 'I am sick, and sullen' – give way to considerably larger sentences:

Help me away, dear Charmian, I shall fall.
It cannot be thus long, the sides of nature
Will not sustain it.

Expression of longing and emotion are controlled by caesura, balance, alliteration and the use of the conjunctive 'but', in her

Eternity was in our lips, and eyes,
Bliss in our brows' bent; none our parts so poor,
But was a race of heaven.

The balance of the middle iambic pentameter line achieved by monosyllable, repetitive 'b' sounds, is paralleled in the second half of the line by the 'o' effect. Lengthy reflective, almost conversational lines, quickly give way to tormented, infuriated, hyperbolic utterances when Cleopatra turns upon the messenger, strikes him, and curses him in II,5. Lines of reflective internal monologue are found after Antony's death at the end of Act IV, and her verse fantasies concerning memories of Antony expressed in images in the second scene of the Act V, are but further examples of her rich, complex poetry.

The first speeches in the play by Antony and Cleopatra express their mutual fascination in a ritual-like verse chant of desire. Like two great operatic singers, they echo one another in short and long lines, rhetorical questions, self-absorption, hyperbole, and oxymoron – a familiar device of Elizabethan love poetry. Antony's assertions about their mutual love are deconstructed by Cleopatra's 'Excellent falsehood,' which casts doubt on his values and motivation. Her scepticism gives way to his typical 'Now for the love of Love, and her soft hours'. This note of contrast is at the heart of the poetry of Antony and Cleopatra and finds its clearest expression in the imagery of the play.

Prose and its functions

Prose in Shakespeare's plays generally represents a social, in addition to a dramatic, contrast, is frequently used by speakers from the lower social backgrounds, and is employed for comedy and parody. Found in non-formal situations, prose is used to indicate comedy and to provide comic relief. In *Antony and Cleopatra* prose alternates with poetry and isn't necessarily restricted to the comic or low-life characters. The Soothsayer uses this in I,2 to contrast with the prose ribaldry of Charmian, Iras and Alexas. Their prose provides a tonal contrast to the Soothsayer's short staccato utterances.

The witty innuendoes serve to deconstruct the Soothsayer's role and convey a different attitude to life, not one of foreboding but one celebrating hedonism. Prose and verse intermingle in the same scene when Antony and Enobarbus talk. Enobarbus's speeches focus upon women. Cleopatra is contrasted with the elements: 'winds and waters sighs and tears ... storms and tempests'; Fulvia with Cleopatra: she is but a tailor's plain smock that has been replaced with a new petticoat, and the 'tears' that Antony sheds for his dead wife merely 'live in an onion'. Enobarbus's prose is complex, literary and sophisticated. Its tone contrasts with Antony's lengthy poetic lines relating to his return to Rome. Enobarbus's prose places Antony's actions in their personal context, Antony's poetry places his action in a public and historical context in which 'Sextus Pompeius/Hath given the dare to Caesar, and commands/The empire of the sea'.

Enobarbus's use of prose in the II,2 may be divided into two sections. First, he interrupts the triumvirs with basic truths, with sharp one-liners such as 'Would we had all such wives, that the men might go to wars with the women'. Antony's rejoinder, shutting Enobarbus up – 'Thou art a soldier only, speak no more' – is a tribute to his percipience, honesty, and lack of pretension. Manipulating politicians do not like too much truth telling. Indeed in *Antony and Cleopatra* poetry is often the vehicle for preposterous suggestions and fantasies – found, for instance, in Enobarbus's verse speech describing Cleopatra on her barge. This speech is prepared for by a prose exchange between Enobarbus, Maecenas and Agrippa and forms the second example of the use of prose in this scene. These three characters are the representatives of the scheming triumvirs. Well satisfied with Antony's agreeing to marry Octavia they have left the stage, which is taken over by three less politically powerful beings. Their comments provide a commentary and wider perspective on events. Egypt, according to Enobarbus, is 'Half the heart of Caesar'; it's the part of the Roman Empire he desires. Enobarbus's account of the way time was spent in Egypt puns on the word 'light', provides a rhyming antithesis between 'night' and 'light', and is poetic in its implications of non-stop entertainment: 'Ay, sir, we did sleep day out of countenance; and made the night light with drinking.'

The prose usage of Enobarbus is far from simple and contains arresting metaphors. When asked by Maecenas if it is true that in Egypt 'Eight wild-boars roasted whole at a breakfast, and but twelve persons there', his reply 'This was but as a fly by an eagle', contains an arresting metaphor of contrast, size, and political implication, the eagle of course being a symbol for Roman Imperial authority. Enobarbus's intitial account of Cleopatra in prose before giving way to poetry succinctly summarizes Antony and Cleopatra's first encounter through the image of capturing his heart: 'When she first met Mark Antony, she purs'd up his heart upon the river of Cydnus'. His image suggests both the closing together of the purse strings, and of heart strings, and conveys the persuasive power Cleopatra has over Mark Antony.

Ribald prose jokes between Enobarbus and Menas punctuate and provide a commentary on the tense confrontation between Caesar, Lepidus, Antony and Pompey (II,6). Antony's rare intrusion into the medium is not without irony. The crocodile had the reputation for weeping over its victims: Lepidus is shortly to be a victim of intrigue; Antony, by the end of the play, will also be a victim. More conventional prose usage is represented by the servants in this banquet scene.

In III,5 prose conveys news and information concerning Caesar's manipulation of Lepidus. In IV,3 the soldiers guarding Cleopatra's palace use prose, which is punctuated by the mysterious sounds of music. In the final scene of the drama the clown, as befits his lowly status, uses prose – which, however, is not without elaborate punning and repetitions on worms and women. Again, his prose has a contrasting function, as it is followed by Cleopatra's impassioned verse packed with meaning and by her dramatic death.

General questions

1 Why is Antony so angry with Thidias?

Suggested notes for essay answer:
Scenic placement of Antony's assault on Thidias and noting of its context. III,13, Antony interrupts Cleopatra's conference with Caesar's ambassador Thidias. Content of Thidias's message and Cleopatra's response – ambiguity. Antony and Enobarbus intrude at a crucial moment: Thidias, Caesar's agent, is kissing Cleopatra's hand. Understandable misunderstood reaction.

Extent of Antony's over-reaction important. Enobarbus indicates in a whispered aside – ''Tis better playing with a lion's whelp,/Than with an old one dying' – that Antony's powers are declining. This confirmed in the repeated orders to whip Thidias, which suggest impotence and diminution of authority in Antony.

Notice Antony's insistence on Thidias's boyishness, his immaturity. Thidias is 'the jack of Caesar'. Thidias becomes the object of Antony's envy of Caesar, his growing power, his youth.

Antony's anger represents his mortality and decline; it exemplifies his dependence upon Cleopatra, who also becomes the object for his insults, suspicions and fears. He focuses upon her sensuous past, her assumed infidelity and disloyalty: she has 'been a boggler ever'. Images of decaying and rotten food and sexual depravity are a reflection of Antony's own decay. The outburst, the result of misunderstanding and misreading of a hand-kiss, reveals Antony's lack of judgement and paranoid state. The violence and force of his metaphors reflect the turbulent emotions within him.

Conclusion: The whipping of Caesar's representative can serve no useful purpose. It can only make things worse for Antony. He is to some extent his own worst enemy, partly responsible for his own decay: hence his anger with Thidias. The decaying lion is aware of his own mortality and his entrapment by Cleopatra.

2 Write an essay on the dramatic treatment of the idea of Egypt in *Antony and Cleopatra*.

3 To what extent do you think that Philo's observation that 'The triple pillar of the world transform'd/Into a strumpet's fool'

indicates the nature of the tragedy of *Antony and Cleopatra*.

4 Discuss Shakespeare's use of his source materials in *Antony and Cleopatra*.

5 How does the structure of *Antony and Cleopatra* reflect its themes?

6 In what ways does the imagery of the play reflect its structure?

7 'The setting of *Antony and Cleopatra* draws attention to its central structural antithesis.' Discuss.

8 Why can 'custom' not 'stale' Cleopatra's 'infinite variety'?

9 '*Antony and Cleopatra* is a play of paradox and contrast.'

10 'Is Antony or we in fault for this?' Use Cleopatra's question as the starting point for a discussion of Antony's character.

11 How true is the observation that Antony's 'taints and honours waged equal with him'?

12 'Caesar is cold, calculating, and ruthless.' Do you agree?

13 What is Enobarbus's role in the play?

14 Write an essay on the poetry of *Antony and Cleopatra*.

15 Why does Octavius Caesar triumph over Antony?

16 In what ways are the themes of loyalty and betrayal reflected in *Antony and Cleopatra*?

17 How would you stage the play and what specific problems do you think its production presents?

18 Comment on Dryden's observation that *Antony and Cleopatra* is concerned with 'the excellency of the moral: For the chief persons represented were famous patterns of unlawful love; and their end accordingly was unfortunate'. Do you agree?

19 Is Dr Johnson correct in his belief that *Antony and Cleopatra*'s 'power of delighting is derived from the frequent changes of the scene'?

20 Why does Cleopatra commit suicide?

21 'The personalities of Antony and Cleopatra are almost irrelevant to the play. What is important are competing value systems, and the attempt of a decaying regime to prevent its disintegration.' Discuss.

22 Is there any light relief in the play?

Further reading

The Common Liar: An Essay on Antony and Cleopatra, J. Adelman (Yale University Press, 1973)

Shakespeare's Language: an introduction, N. F. Blake, (Macmillan London, 1983).

Shakespeare Antony and Cleopatra A Casebook, J. Russell Brown, ed., (London Macmillan, 1968). Contains extracts from Bradley, Dryden, Johnson, Coleridge, Hazlitt, H. Granville Barker and others.

Narrative and Dramatic Source of Shakespeare, Vol. 5 The Roman Plays, G. Bullough (London, Routledge and Kegan Paul, 1964). Contains *Plutarch's Lives of Noble Grecians and Romans*.

Shakespeare's Roman Plays, M. Charney (Cambridge, Mass., Harvard University Press, 1961).

Antony and Cleopatra and All For Love in *The Living Principle*, F. R. Leavis (London, Chatto & Windus, 1975).

Shakespeare's Bawdy, E. Partridge (London, Routledge and Kegan Paul, rev. and enlarged ed., 1968).

Antony and Cleopatra and the Book of Revelation, Review of English Studies, E. Seaton (1946), 219–224.

Shakespeare's Imagery and What it tells us, C. Spurgeon (Cambridge University Press 1935).

An Approach to Shakespeare, D. A. Traversi, Second ed., (London, Sands & Co., 1957).